1st EDITION

Perspectives on Modern World History

The Montgomery Bus Boycott

1st EDITION

Perspectives on Modern World History

The Montgomery Bus Boycott

Jeff Hay

Editor

GREENHAVEN PRESS
A part of Gale, Cengage Learning

GALE
CENGAGE Learning·

Detroit • New York • San Francisco • New Haven, Conn • Waterville, Maine • London

Elizabeth Des Chenes, *Managing Editor*

© 2012 Greenhaven Press, a part of Gale, Cengage Learning.

Gale and Greenhaven Press are registered trademarks used herein under license.

For more information, contact:
Greenhaven Press
27500 Drake Rd.
Farmington Hills, MI 48331-3535
Or you can visit our Internet site at gale.cengage.com.

For product information and technology assistance, contact us at
Gale Customer Support, 1-800-877-4253.

For permission to use material from this text or product, submit all requests online at
www.cengage.com/permissions.

Further permissions questions can be e-mailed to permissionrequest@cengage.com.

Articles in Greenhaven Press anthologies are often edited for length to meet page requirements. In addition, original titles of these works are changed to clearly present the main thesis and to explicitly indicate the author's opinion. Every effort is made to ensure that Greenhaven Press accurately reflects the original intent of the authors. Every effort has been made to trace the owners of copyrighted material.

Cover image © Everett Collection Inc./Alamy; © Bettmann/Corbis.

LIBRARY OF CONGRESS CATALOGING-IN-PUBLICATION DATA

The Montgomery Bus Boycott / Jeff T. Hay, book editor.
   p. cm. -- (Perspectives on modern world history)
   Includes bibliographical references and index.
   ISBN 978-0-7377-5795-8 (hardcover)
1. Montgomery Bus Boycott, Montgomery, Ala., 1955–1956. 2. African Americans--Civil rights--Alabama--Montgomery--History--20th century. 3. Segregation in transportation--Alabama--Montgomery--History--20th century. 4. Civil rights movements--Alabama--Montgomery--History--20th century. 5. Montgomery (Ala.)--Race relations--History--20th century. I. Hay, Jeff.
   F334.M79N455 2012
   323.1196'073076147--dc23

          2011024550

Printed in the United States of America
1 2 3 4 5 6 7 15 14 13 12 11

CONTENTS

J. Mills Thornton III

In December 1955, an African American seamstress and activist named Rosa Parks refused to give up her seat on a Montgomery, Alabama, public bus to a white man, as local law required. Her arrest sparked a citywide boycott of Montgomery buses that attracted nationwide attention.

U•X•L Encyclopedia of U.S. History

From 1954 to 1965, African American activists and tens of thousands of ordinary citizens of all ethnic backgrounds took part in a nationwide civil rights movement that helped result in new laws guaranteeing equality. Events such as the Montgomery Bus Boycott were major signposts in the movement by helping, among other things, to make famous such leaders as Dr. Martin Luther King, Jr.

CHAPTER 2 | **Controversies Connected to the Montgomery Bus Boycott**

pastor, used his training in and commitment to nonviolent protest tactics in his leadership of the bus boycott and later civil rights efforts.

CHAPTER 3   Personal Narratives

FOREWORD

*"History cannot give us a program for the future,
but it can give us a fuller understanding of ourselves, and of our common humanity, so that we
can better face the future."*
— *Robert Penn Warren,*
American poet and novelist

The history of each nation is punctuated by momentous events that represent turning points for that
nation, with an impact felt far beyond its borders.
These events—displaying the full range of human capa-
bilities, from violence, greed, and ignorance to heroism,
courage, and strength—are nearly always complicated
and multifaceted. Any student of history faces the challenge of grasping the many strands that constitute such
world-changing events as wars, social movements, and
environmental disasters. But understanding these significant historic events can be enhanced by exposure to
a variety of perspectives, whether of people involved in-
timately or of ones observing from a distance of miles or
years. Understanding can also be increased by learning
about the controversies surrounding such events and ex-
ploring hot-button issues from multiple angles. Finally,
true understanding of important historic events involves
knowledge of the events' human impact—of the ways
such events affected people in their everyday lives—all
over the world.

Perspectives on Modern World History examines
global historic events from the twentieth-century onward
by presenting analysis and observation from numerous
vantage points. Each volume offers high school, early
college level, and general interest readers a thematically

1

arranged anthology of previously published materials that address a major historical event, with an emphasis on international coverage. Each volume opens with background information on the event, then presents the controversies surrounding that event, and concludes with first-person narratives from people who lived through the event or were affected by it. By providing primary sources from the time of the event, as well as relevant commentary surrounding the event, this series can be used to inform debate, help develop critical thinking skills, increase global awareness, and enhance an understanding of international perspectives on history.

Material in each volume is selected from a diverse range of sources, including journals, magazines, newspapers, nonfiction books, personal narratives, speeches, congressional testimony, government documents, pamphlets, organization newsletters, and position papers. Articles taken from these sources are carefully edited and introduced to provide context and background. Each volume of Perspectives on Modern World History includes an array of views on events of global significance. Much of the material comes from international sources and from US sources that provide extensive international coverage.

Each volume in the Perspectives on Modern World History series also includes:

- A full-color **world map**, offering context and geographic perspective.
- An annotated **table of contents** that provides a brief summary of each essay in the volume.
- An **introduction** specific to the volume topic.
- For each viewpoint, a brief **introduction** that has notes about the author and source of the viewpoint, and that provides a summary of its main points.
- Full-color **charts**, **graphs**, **maps**, and other visual representations.

- Informational **sidebars** that explore the lives of key individuals, give background on historical events, or explain scientific or technical concepts.
- A **glossary** that defines key terms, as needed.
- A **chronology** of important dates preceding, during, and immediately following the event.
- A **bibliography** of additional books, periodicals, and websites for further research.
- A comprehensive **subject index** that offers access to people, places, and events cited in the text.

Perspectives on Modern World History is designed for a broad spectrum of readers who want to learn more about not only history but also current events, political science, government, international relations, and sociology—students doing research for class assignments or debates, teachers and faculty seeking to supplement course materials, and others wanting to improve their understanding of history. Each volume of Perspectives on Modern World History is designed to illuminate a complicated event, to spark debate, and to show the human perspective behind the world's most significant happenings of recent decades.

INTRODUCTION

Until the middle of the twentieth century, in many parts of the United States, African Americans could be segregated legally from white Americans in public places. States, cities, and towns had the legal right to establish "separate but equal" facilities under an 1896 Supreme Court decision, *Plessy v. Ferguson*. Private businesses and other institutions had the same rights. Parks, restaurants, movie theaters, buses and trains, entrances to such public buildings as town halls and courts, even water fountains could be legally labeled "whites only" and, as it was commonly put decades ago, "colored only." Segregation even persisted in public schools and, on a national level, in the armed forces. Often, and especially in southern states where they were quite common, rules segregating blacks and whites were known as "Jim Crow."

The Montgomery Bus Boycott of 1955 to 1956 was a key event in helping to bring these segregation laws to an end. The boycott occurred at the beginning of a decade of intensive civil rights protests that captured the attention and sympathy of much of the nation and the world. In addition, events in Montgomery, Alabama, provided the stage on which important civil rights leaders emerged, notably Dr. Martin Luther King Jr., and they helped make an unassuming Montgomery woman, Rosa Parks, a household name. Finally, the boycott showed the power of passive, nonviolent resistance in bringing about social change.

Before the 1950s, many of the challenges to Jim Crow took the form of localized court cases, but most had little impact. A brief 1953 boycott of public transportation in Baton Rouge, Louisiana, for instance, merely resulted in

African Americans gaining access to a few more seats. In 1948, meanwhile, an important transition took place when, by executive order, President Harry S. Truman ordered the integration of the armed forces in the face of much opposition from service leaders. The effective beginning of the civil rights movement, however, was a decision reached by the US Supreme Court in 1954. Known as *Brown v. Board of Education*, the decision overturned *Plessy v. Ferguson* and ruled that segregation in American public schools was unconstitutional. Civil rights leaders and activists now had a legal foundation by which to challenge other forms of segregation.

The city of Montgomery, Alabama's capital, was home to many such activists and contained a large African American population. Many of them relied on buses to get to work or school, to downtown shops, and to other destinations. Montgomery's bus company, National City Lines, was privately owned and operated and maintained a complicated system of rules to separate black and white riders. Most simply, blacks had to sit at the back, and generally enter the bus through a rear door, even after stepping into and then out of front doors to pay their fare. Once buses were full, white riders could demand seats from black riders, who then had to stand. From time to time, black riders might refuse to abandon their seats; they often suffered insults from drivers in any case. Those who refused to give up their seats could then be arrested under city ordinances that gave bus drivers the freedom to assign seats. This fate was suffered in March 1955 by Claudette Colvin, a fifteen-year-old high school girl from one of Montgomery's poorer neighborhoods.

At that point, some of Montgomery's activists had their eyes and ears open for an incident that might provide the basis for a court challenge to segregation on the city's buses. These activists included Jo Ann Robinson, a professor at Alabama State College and a member of the Women's Political Council, as well as E.D. Dixon, the head of the local chapter of the National Association for the Advancement of Colored People (NAACP). Dixon and other activists came to the conclusion that Claudette Colvin's case would not make an effective focus for a legal challenge, especially after the young girl was discovered to be pregnant and refused to name the father of the child.

On December 1, 1955, another Montgomery woman refused to give up her seat when asked by the driver to do so. This woman was Rosa Parks, tired after a long day at work and, ironically, finding herself face-to-face with a driver she always tried to avoid because of earlier conflicts. Parks, like Colvin, was eventually arrested and, after a few hours in jail, was bailed out by Dixon and Clifford Durr, a white lawyer.

Rosa Parks, then forty-two years old, was well-known to Dixon and other activists as the secretary of the NAACP. Her dignified, unassuming manner reinforced their sense that she might be an effective face at the center of a protest against bus segregation. Parks pledged to cooperate, and Robinson set to work immediately to publicize plans for a one-day boycott of Montgomery buses to take place on Monday, December 5. The boycott was a huge success and, at a meeting held that evening at a local church, large crowds pledged to continue the boycott. It was at this meeting that Reverend Martin Luther King Jr., pastor at Dexter Avenue Baptist Church in Montgomery, stepped forward as the leader of the growing protest. King, Robinson, Dixon, and others formed the Montgomery Improvement Association (MIA) not only to lead the boycott, but to engage in negotiations with city and bus company officials and prepare court challenges.

The Montgomery Bus Boycott lasted more than a year. During that period the city's African Americans adjusted by taking fewer trips, walking, riding bikes, and using a carpool network organized by the MIA and church groups; few could afford their own cars. City officials refused to negotiate major concessions, and it was only a major lawsuit, *Browder v. Gayle*, that brought any sort of conclusion to the event. The case, first decided in June 1956 at the district court level by a panel of three Alabama judges, determined that bus segregation was indeed unconstitutional. The two judges who made the majority ruling cited *Brown v. Board of Education* as a precedent. Montgomery officials appealed the case all the way to the US Supreme Court, which in November 1956 upheld the district court's determination. Once the decision was implemented in late December, the boycott came to an end, and Montgomery's African Americans started riding buses once again.

A major reason for the success of the boycott, as well as for the attention and sympathy it drew from around the world, was that the event was built around passive resistance, nonviolence, and legal challenges. African American leaders generally understood that the use of violence would only work against them, and even before the boycott began Rosa Parks and others were already getting training in nonviolent tactics. Martin Luther King Jr., for his part, emerged as the strongest and most articulate advocate of such measures. Even after his home was bombed in January 1956, and while threats and attacks continued for the rest of the year, King urged protesters to refrain from violence and maintain their pride and dignity. Similarly, King argued, protesters should suffer arrest and punishment calmly, as he himself did when he was arrested and charged, along with other boycott leaders, for violating an obscure city ordinance in February 1956.

King's fame grew when, after the Montgomery boycott ended in success, he formed the Southern Christian Leadership Conference (SCLC). The organization was often at the center of civil rights protests in the coming years, including such events as sit-ins in places like

Selma, Alabama, and mass gatherings such as the 1963 March on Washington. Throughout, King continued to rely on tactics designed to change people's minds and hearts, as opposed to simply defeating his opponents. By using such means, and despite his untimely assassination in 1968, King rose from being a young Montgomery pastor in 1955 to becoming one of the most influential figures in American history.

Jim Crow finally came to an end with the 1964 Civil Rights Act. Signed by US president Lyndon B. Johnson fewer than ten years after the Montgomery Bus Boycott began, the act made it illegal for public and most private institutions to discriminate on the basis of race, ethnicity, gender, or religion. Rosa Parks's simple statement of "no" during a late afternoon bus ride on December 1, 1955, was a major spark in making the Civil Rights Act a reality. Her influence even spread overseas, helping to inspire a bus boycott in Bristol, England, in 1963. Parks, who passed away in 2005, was named one of the most influential people of the twentieth century by *Time* magazine, and the bus where she made her quiet stand is maintained in a museum near Detroit, Michigan, the city where Parks spent the last years of her life.

World Map

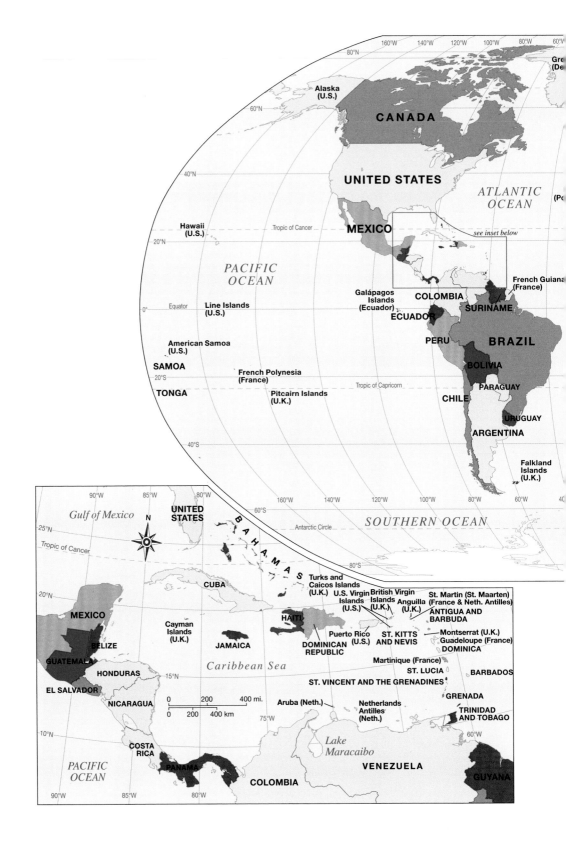

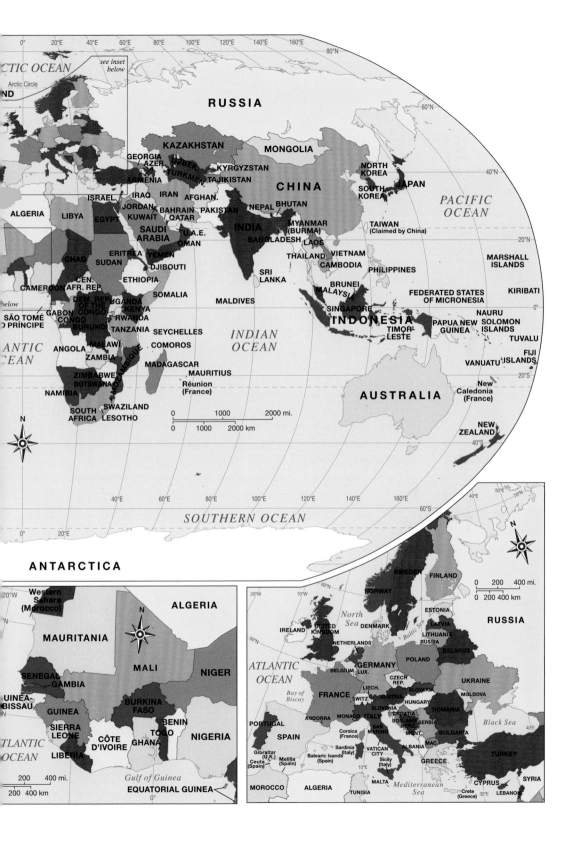

CHAPTER 1

The History of the Montgomery Bus Boycott

An Overview of the Montgomery Bus Boycott

J. Mills Thornton III

A boycott of city buses in Montgomery, Alabama, began in December 1955 and lasted just over a year. The following overview examines how the refusal of local woman Rosa Parks to give up her seat on a city bus, as Montgomery law then required, crystallized years of frustration among the city's African American community. Both leaders and ordinary citizens united to challenge Parks's arrest, and they quickly agreed to a boycott of the city's buses. The efforts of one leader, a newly arrived Baptist minister named Martin Luther King Jr., helped to ensure that the protest remained both dignified and nonviolent despite many challenges and threats. The boycott ended, the author notes, after the US Supreme Court upheld a lower court ruling that segregation on the city's buses was unconstitutional. The boycott's legacy included a short wave of violence, an expansion in national awareness of the

Photo on previous page: The restored bus where Rosa Parks was arrested for refusing to give up her seat to a white man is on permanent display at the Henry Ford Museum in Dearborn, Michigan. (**Bill Pugliano/ Stringer/Getty Images.**) Walking to work

SOURCE. J. Mills Thornton III, "Montgomery, Ala. Bus Boycott," *Encyclopedia of African-American Culture and History*, Colin A. Palmer, ed. Belmont, CA: Macmillan Reference USA, 2006, pp. 1471–1474. Copyright © 2006 Gale, Cengage Learning. All rights reserved. Reproduced by permission of Gale, a part of Cengage Learning.

burgeoning civil rights movement, and the emergence of King as a central figure in that movement. J. Mills Thornton III is a professor of history at the University of Michigan and the author of *Politics and Power in a Slave Society*.

T he Montgomery Bus Boycott began on December 5, 1955, as an effort by black residents to protest the trial that day in the Montgomery [Alabama] Recorder's Court of Rosa McCauley Parks. She had been arrested on December 1 for violating the city's ordinance requiring racial segregation of seating on buses. The boycott had initially been intended to last only for the single day of the trial, but local black support of the strike proved so great that, at a meeting that afternoon, black community leaders decided to continue the boycott until city and bus company authorities met black demands for (1) the adoption by the bus company in Montgomery of the pattern of seating segregation used by the same company in Mobile; (2) the hiring of black bus drivers on predominantly black routes; and (3) greater courtesy by drivers toward passengers. The leaders formed the Montgomery Improvement Association (MIA) to run the extended boycott. At a mass meeting that evening, several thousand blacks ratified these decisions.

The Mobile plan sought by the boycott differed from the Montgomery pattern in that passengers, once seated, could not be unseated by drivers. In Mobile, blacks seated from the back and whites from the front, but after the bus was full, the racial division could be adjusted only when riders disembarked. On Montgomery's buses, the front ten seats were irrevocably reserved for whites, whether or not there were any whites aboard, and the rear ten seats were in theory similarly reserved for blacks. The racial designation of the middle sixteen seats, however, was adjusted by the drivers to accord with the changing racial composition of the ridership as the bus proceeded along its route. In Rosa Parks's case, when she had taken her seat, it had been in the black section of the bus. Two blocks further on, all the white seats and the white standing room were taken, but some standing room remained in the rear. The bus driver, J. Fred Blake, then ordered the row of seats in which Parks was sitting cleared to make room for boarding whites. Three blacks complied, but Mrs. Parks refused and was arrested. She was fined fourteen dollars.

Longtime Frustrations

Black Montgomerians had long been dissatisfied with the form of bus segregation used in their city. It had originally been adopted for streetcars in August 1900, and had provoked a boycott that had lasted for almost two years. In October 1952 a delegation from the black Women's Political Council had urged the city commission to permit the use of the Mobile seating plan. In a special election in the fall of 1953, a racial liberal with strong black support, Dave Birmingham, was elected to the three-member city commission. Following his inauguration, blacks again pressed the seating proposal at meetings in December 1953 and March 1954, though to no avail. In May 1954, the president of the Women's Political Council, Jo Ann G. Robinson, a professor of English at Alabama State College for Negroes, wrote to the mayor to warn that blacks might launch a boycott if white authorities continued to be adamant. During the municipal election in the spring of 1955, black leaders held a candidates' forum at which they posed questions about issues of interest to the black community. At the head of the list was the adoption of the Mobile seating pattern.

On March 2, only weeks before the election, a black teenager, Claudette Colvin, was arrested for violation of

> " Black Montgomerians had long been dissatisfied with the form of bus segregation used in their city. "

was the choice for many during the bus boycott. (Grey Villet/ Contributor/Time & Life Pictures/Getty Images.)

the bus segregation ordinance. Following this incident, representatives of the city and the bus company promised black negotiators that a seating policy more favorable to African Americans would be adopted. However, Dave Birmingham, the racially liberal city commissioner elected in 1953, had integrated the city police force in 1954. As a result of hostility to this action and other similar ones, he was defeated for reelection in 1955 by an outspoken segregationist, Clyde Sellers. The other commissioners at once became less accommodating. By the time that Rosa Parks was arrested in December, the discussions had come to a standstill. Mrs. Parks, the secretary of the Montgomery branch of the National Association for the Advancement of Colored People (NAACP), shared with other black leaders the frustration that grew out of the negotiations with municipal authorities. This frustration produced her refusal to vacate her seat.

From the city jail, Parks telephoned Edgar D. Nixon, a Pullman porter [railway employee] who was a former president of the Montgomery NAACP branch. After Nixon had posted bail for Parks, he called other prominent blacks to propose the one-day boycott. The response was generally positive. At Jo Ann Robinson's suggestion, the Women's Political Council immediately began distributing leaflets urging the action. It was then endorsed by the city's black ministers and other leaders at a meeting at the Dexter Avenue Baptist Church. The result was almost universal black participation.

Ready for a Boycott

At the December 5 meeting, when it was decided to continue the boycott and to form the Montgomery Improvement Association (MIA), the Reverend Dr. Martin Luther King Jr. was chosen as the MIA's president, principally because, as a young man who had lived in the city only fifteen months, he was not as yet involved in the bitter rivalry for leadership of the black community between Nixon and Rufus A. Lewis, a funeral director. Nixon was elected the MIA's treasurer, and Lewis was appointed to organize car pools to transport blacks to their jobs without having to use buses. The Reverend Ralph D. Abernathy was named to head the committee designated to reopen negotiations with the city and the bus company.

Initially, the renewed negotiations seemed promising. Mayor William A. Gayle asked a committee of white community leaders to meet with the MIA's delegates. But by January 1956, these discussions had reached a stalemate. The MIA's attorney, Fred D. Gray, urged that the MIA abandon its request for the Mobile plan in favor of filing a federal court lawsuit seeking to declare unconstitutional all forms of seating segregation. The MIA's executive board resisted this proposal until January 30, when Martin Luther King's home was bombed. On the next day, the executive board voted to authorize the suit, which was filed as *Browder v. Gayle* on February 1.

Meanwhile, similar strains were at work in the white community. A group of moderate businessmen, the Men of Montgomery, was attempting to mediate between the MIA and the city commission. But segregationists were pressing authorities to seek the indictment of the boycott's leaders in state court for violating the Alabama Anti-Boycott Act of 1921, which made it a misdemeanor to conspire to hinder any person from carrying on a lawful business. On February 20, an MIA mass meeting rejected the compromise proposals of the Men of Montgomery, and on February 21, the county grand jury returned indictments of eighty-nine blacks, twenty-four of whom were ministers, under the Anti-Boycott Act.

Legal Challenges

Martin Luther King, the first to be brought to trial, was convicted by Judge Eugene Carter at the end of March and was fined $500. King appealed, and the remainder of the prosecutions were suspended while the appellate courts considered his case. On May 11, a three-judge federal court heard *Browder v. Gayle* and on June 5, in an opinion by Circuit Judge Richard Rives, it ruled two to one that any law requiring racially segregated seating on buses violated the equal protection clause of the Constitution's Fourteenth Amendment. The city appealed to the U.S. Supreme Court. Both segregation and the boycott continued while the appeal was pending.

> Throughout the thirteen months of negotiations and legal maneuvers, the boycott was sustained by mass meetings and its car-pool operation.

Throughout the thirteen months of negotiations and legal maneuvers, the boycott was sustained by mass meetings and its car-pool operation. The weekly mass meetings, rotated among the city's black churches, continually reinforced the high level of emotional commitment to the movement among the black population. The car pool, modeled on one used during a brief bus boycott in Baton Rouge [Louisiana] in 1953, initially consisted of private cars whose owners volunteered to participate. But as contributions flowed in from sympathetic northerners, the MIA eventually purchased a fleet of station wagons, assigned ownership of them to the various black churches, hired drivers, and established regular routes. Rufus Lewis administered the car pool until May 1956, when he was succeeded by the Rev. B.J. Simms.

White authorities eventually realized that the MIA's ability to perpetuate the boycott depended on its successful organization of the car pool. In November the city sued in state court for an injunction to forbid the carpool operation on the ground that it was infringing on the bus company's exclusive franchise. On November 13, Judge Eugene Carter granted the injunction, and the car pool ceased operation the next day. But on that same day, the U.S. Supreme Court summarily affirmed the previous ruling of the lower federal court that bus segregation was unconstitutional. The city petitioned the Supreme Court for rehearing, and a final order was delayed until December 20. On December 21, 1956, the buses were integrated and the boycott ended.

A Violent Aftermath to Victory

The city was at once plunged into violence. Snipers fired into the buses, with one of the shots shattering the leg of a pregnant black passenger, Rosa Jordan. The city commission ordered the suspension of night bus service. On January 10, 1957, four black churches and the homes of the Reverend Ralph Abernathy and of the MIA's only white board member, the Reverend Robert Graetz, were bombed and heavily damaged. All bus service was then suspended. On January 27, a home near that of Martin

Luther King was bombed and destroyed, and a bomb at King's own home was defused. On January 30, Montgomery police arrested seven bombers, all of whom were members of the Ku Klux Klan.

The arrests ended the violence, and in March full bus service resumed. However, the first two of the bombers to come to trial were acquitted in May 1957, despite their confessions and the irrefutable evidence against them. Meanwhile, in April, the Alabama Court of Appeals had affirmed on technical grounds King's conviction under the Anti-Boycott Act. Because it was now clear that the other bombing prosecutions would be unsuccessful, and because the boycott had ended in any case, prosecutors in November agreed to dismiss all the remaining bombing and anti-boycott-law indictments in return for King's payment of his $500 fine.

> The Montgomery Bus Boycott marked the beginning of the civil rights movement's direct action phase, and it made Martin Luther King Jr. a national figure.

The Montgomery Bus Boycott marked the beginning of the civil rights movement's direct action phase, and it made Martin Luther King Jr. a national figure. Although the integration of the buses was actually produced by the federal court injunction rather than by the boycott, it was the boycott that began the process of moving the civil rights movement out of the courtroom by demonstrating that ordinary African Americans possessed the power to control their own destiny.

The Montgomery Bus Boycott Was a Key Moment in the Civil Rights Movement

U·X·L Encyclopedia of U.S. History

The status of African Americans changed dramatically because of the civil rights movement of the 1950s and 1960s. The following selection summarizes the major aspects and developments of the movement and provides a brief background. The Montgomery Bus Boycott of 1955 and 1956 was one of the early turning points of the civil rights movement, galvanizing support and attracting attention nationwide. It also allowed Dr. Martin Luther King Jr. to emerge as an important civil rights leader and advocate of nonviolent resistance. The boycott quickly followed the US Supreme Court's 1954 decision in *Brown v. Board of Education* that segregation in public schools was unconstitutional. The efforts of Dr. King and millions of others, in the face of much resistance, finally resulted in

---

SOURCE. "Civil Rights Movement (1954–1965)," *U•X•L Encyclopedia of U.S. History*. Belmont, CA: UXL, 2009, pp. 302–308. Copyright © 2009 Gale, Cengage Learning. All rights reserved. Reproduced by permission of Gale, a part of Cengage Learning.

broad civil rights and voting rights legislation enacted in 1964 and 1965. The selection notes that the movement turned increasingly violent after that, with one of its saddest events being the 1968 assassination of Dr. King. The authors also state that, even in recent years, the effort to ensure equality and fairness continues.

The American civil rights struggle is an ongoing fight for the personal rights, protections, and privileges granted all U.S. citizens by the Constitution and Bill of Rights. At the end of the American Civil War (1861–65), constitutional amendments were enacted to protect African Americans recently released from slavery. The Fourteenth Amendment (1868) declared that all former slaves were U.S. citizens and received equal protection under the laws of state and federal governments. The Fifteenth Amendment (1870) assured equal voting rights to all citizens, regardless of race. Until the 1950s, however, the civil rights of African Americans were systematically denied, particularly in the South where the majority of black Americans resided. A remarkable era of nonviolent African American activism began in 1954, known today simply as the civil rights movement. It was launched by the *Brown v. Board of Education* decision in 1954, in which the Supreme Court ruled that segregation in the public schools was illegal. This phase of the civil rights struggle ended with the passage in 1965 of the Voting Rights Act, which—nearly a century after the Fifteenth Amendment had already done so—once again assured voting rights to all citizens.

Background of the Movement

After the Reconstruction Era (1865–77), a period after the Civil War in which the federal government controlled the southern states that had seceded (withdrawn) from the Union, whites in the South enacted the Jim Crow laws. These were a series of laws throughout the South that required segregation, the separation of the races in public places. White southern state legislatures limited African American rights to own land, to enter certain occupations, and to gain access to the courts. By 1900, southern whites had accomplished the disfranchisement (exclusion from voting) of most southern blacks.

In the early twentieth century, because it was too dangerous to effectively resist racial injustice in the South, most civil rights struggles were carried out in the North. In 1905, black scholar and author W.E.B. Du Bois (1868–1963) and other black leaders began the Niagara movement, named after their meeting place near the Niagara River bordering the United States and Canada, to fight racial injustice. Their organization eventually became the National Association for the Advancement of Colored People (NAACP), which fought for racial equality mainly through the courts and the press. Until World War II (1939–45), the NAACP's progress was slow.

> Southern congressmen and governors vowed to resist desegregation.

After the war, a new sense of urgency prevailed in American black communities. Soldiers who had risked their lives to fight for the country expected equal treatment when they returned home. More than one million African Americans migrated from the rural South to northern cities in the first decades of the century. Over two million blacks had registered to vote by the late 1940s. In December 1948, President Harry S. Truman (1884–1972; served 1945–53) ran for his second term as president on a strong civil rights plank. Although some southern whites quickly abandoned him, he received 70 percent of the northern black vote and won the election. Two years later, he began to desegregate the armed forces.

By the late 1940s, the NAACP's chief legal counsel, Thurgood Marshall (1908–1993), brought the principle

National Guardsmen were deployed to guard Freedom Riders as they tested bus integration laws throughout the South. (Paul Schutzer/ Contributor/Time & Life Pictures/Getty Images.)

of segregation in public education before the Supreme Court. Marshall argued that segregation denied blacks equal protection of the laws as guaranteed by the Fourteenth Amendment to the Constitution. In 1954, the Supreme Court unanimously ruled against segregation in public schools in *Brown v. Board of Education*.

The Aftermath of *Brown*

Brown's most immediate effect was to intensify the resistance of white southerners to civil rights progress. The Ku Klux Klan, a secret society of white southerners in the United States that uses terrorist tactics to suppress African Americans and other minorities, stepped up its violent intimidation of African Americans. Southern congressmen and governors vowed to resist desegregation. In 1957, when nine black students attempted to attend classes at a formerly all-white school in Little Rock, Arkansas, federal troops were required to protect them from the furious white mobs.

Even so, *Brown* provided the spark that ignited a movement. African Americans across the country recognized that the highest court had upheld their rights; leaders began to prepare bolder assaults on segregation in the South. One common form of protest is a boycott, an organized refusal to do business with someone. In December 1955, blacks in Montgomery, Alabama, organized a bus boycott after the former NAACP secretary of the Montgomery branch, Rosa Parks (1913–2005), was arrested for refusing to yield her seat to a white man. The boycott leader was Martin Luther King Jr. (1929–1968). Only twenty-six years old, the minister from Atlanta was an inspiring speaker who invoked Christian morality, American ideals of liberty, and the ethic of nonviolent resistance in his campaign against racial injustice. In November 1956, despite growing white violence, the bus boycott triumphed when a Supreme Court decision overturned Montgomery's laws enforcing bus segregation.

Nonviolent Activists Organize

In 1957, Congress passed the first Civil Rights Act since the Reconstruction Era. African Americans, however, had seen that court decisions and federal acts had consistently failed to make changes, so during the late 1950s they moved their struggle for equality to the streets. In January 1957, King organized the Southern Christian Leadership Conference (SCLC), a network of nonviolent civil rights activists drawn mainly from African American churches.

In 1960, four African American students began the sit-in movement, when they sat at the lunch counter at

> "Protesters courageously endured insults, intimidation, violence, and arrest without striking back."

a Woolworth's store in Greensboro, North Carolina, which served only whites. The store closed down the lunch counter. Later that year, several hundred student activists gathered in Raleigh, North Carolina, to form the Student Nonviolent Coordinating Committee (SNCC) to promote nonviolent resistance to Jim Crow laws. By the summer of 1960, the sit-ins had desegregated dozens of lunch counters and other public accommodations, mainly in southern border states. Guided by King and other nonviolent activist leaders, protesters courageously endured insults, intimidation, violence, and arrest without striking back.

The Kennedy Administration

Black protests intensified during the presidency of John F. Kennedy (1917–1963; served 1961–63), a Democrat elected in 1960 with heavy black support. Kennedy had started out his administration avoiding civil rights measures that might trigger southern white racial violence and political retaliation. Civil rights leaders stepped up campaigns to pressure Kennedy to fulfill his campaign promises. In 1961, a nonviolent civil rights group called the Congress of Racial Equality (CORE) organized the freedom rides, in which volunteers rode buses through the South, testing compliance with a Supreme Court order to desegregate interstate bus terminal facilities. White mobs beat the riders in Birmingham and Montgomery, Alabama. As several hundred more volunteers stepped in to continue the project, Kennedy quietly persuaded southern communities to desegregate their bus terminals.

In 1962, Kennedy again was forced into action. He sent federal marshals to protect a black student named James Meredith (1933–), who had registered at the all-white University of Mississippi at Oxford. After mobs killed two people at the campus and besieged the marshals, the president reluctantly called in more troops to restore order.

In 1963, demonstrations throughout the South led to fifteen thousand arrests and widespread white violence. On May 3 and for several days afterward, police in Birmingham beat and unleashed attack dogs on nonviolent followers of King, in full view of television news cameras. The resulting public revulsion over the Birmingham protests spurred Kennedy to urge Congress to enact a strong civil rights law.

"I Have a Dream"

A coalition of African American groups and their white allies sponsored a march on Washington, D.C., on August 28, 1963, to advance the civil rights bill then before Congress. Standing before the Lincoln Memorial, King delivered his famous plea for interracial brotherhood in his "I Have a Dream" speech, enthralling several hundred thousand blacks and whites.

On July 2, 1964, President Lyndon B. Johnson (1908–1973; served 1963–69) signed the Civil Rights Act of 1964, which barred segregation in public accommodations, ended federal aid to segregated institutions, outlawed racial discrimination in employment, sought to strengthen black voting rights, and extended the life of the U.S. Commission on Civil Rights.

Voting Rights in the South

In 1964, SNCC initiated Freedom Summer, a massive black voter registration and education campaign aimed at challenging white supremacy in the deep South, starting in Mississippi. About one thousand college students, most of them white, volunteered. The freedom workers were not well received by a segment of Mississippi's white population. Three volunteers were murdered by a mob led by the deputy sheriff of a Mississippi town. Nevertheless, the project continued.

In 1965, King led a march from Selma to Montgomery, Alabama, to extend voting rights to black Americans. State and local police almost immediately attacked the black marchers, stopping the march. The televised scenes of violence brought about strong national support for the protection of blacks attempting to vote. Ten days later, twenty-five thousand black and white marchers reached Montgomery escorted by federal troops.

After the Selma-Montgomery march, Johnson signed a strong Voting Rights Act, which authorized the attorney general to send federal voting examiners to make sure that African Americans were free to register. The examiners were granted the power to enforce national law over local regulations wherever discrimination occurred.

Black Power

After 1965, the civil rights movement began to fragment, primarily over the nonviolent tactics of King and his supporters and the goal of integration into the dominant society. Malcolm X (1925–1965), a leader of the religious and sociopolitical group the Nation of Islam, questioned the value of integration into a society that had exploited and abused African Americans for centuries. He did not believe that the sit-ins, marches, or other tactics of civil rights activists were effective tools with which to gain rights, especially when confronted with violent resistance in the South. In 1966, SNCC leader Stokely Carmichael (also known as Kwame Ture; 1941–1998) ridiculed nonviolent efforts and demanded "black power," a militant slogan that alienated white liberals and divided blacks. The focus of the Black Power Movement began to shift to economic injustices in the

> The central goal of the African American civil rights movement—full equality between blacks and whites—remains a distant vision.

Jim Crow

The roots of the Montgomery Bus Boycott lay in decades of "Jim Crow" laws that segregated blacks and whites in southern states. City buses, like those in Montgomery, Alabama, provided only one example of facilities where these laws assured that blacks and whites were kept separate and in their assigned places, with whites almost always having better access and privileges. Other places included restaurants, parks, and bathrooms. Many public buildings had separate entrances for blacks. Sometimes, signs were even posted over water fountains saying "whites only" or "colored only." Even in institutions fundamental to American life, such as public schools and the military, blacks and whites were segregated. The term "Jim Crow" is thought to have come from an insult directed toward blacks as early as the 1830s and 1840s.

Jim Crow laws arose in the southern United States in the years after the Civil War (1861–1865), mostly after 1875. Many white Southerners resented the emancipation of slaves that the Civil War made possible, and they put in place measures to provide for continued white supremacy in the South. Perhaps the most basic Jim Crow laws were measures to deny blacks the right to vote through literacy tests, poll taxes, or other requirements that the vast majority of poor blacks were unable to meet. Meanwhile, no national laws existed requiring the equal treatment of blacks and whites, so southern governments could easily enact Jim Crow measures. When a rule segregating blacks and whites on Louisiana railroads was tested in the 1890s, the challenge ultimately reached the US Supreme Court. The Court's 1896 decision, *Plessy v. Ferguson*, legalized the ability to create "separate but equal" facilities for blacks and whites and institutionalized Jim Crow across the South.

Legal challenges continued, and in 1948 the US military was integrated by executive order of President Harry S. Truman. Then, in 1954, the Supreme Court returned its decision in *Brown v. Board of Education*. The ruling found that requiring segregation in public schools was unconstitutional and provided a strong foundation for such new challenges as the Montgomery Bus Boycott. The principle of "separate but equal," and any remaining Jim Crow measures, came to an end in 1964 with the passage of a broad, national Civil Rights Act.

North. Violent ghetto riots began to break out in large cities like Detroit and Los Angeles. On April 4, 1968, the assassination of Martin Luther King Jr. touched off riots that left Washington, D.C., in flames for three days. The movement would continue, but this initial remarkable phase of the nonviolent civil rights struggle was over.

A Revolutionary Movement

The central goal of the African American civil rights movement—full equality between blacks and whites—remains a distant vision. Neighborhoods, private schools, and jobs remain segregated along racial lines; African American incomes remain significantly lower than those of whites; and job and educational opportunities are not distributed equally. Nonetheless, the civil rights movement of 1954–65 transformed American race relations. In communities throughout the South, "whites only" signs that had stood for generations vanished from hotels, restrooms, theaters, and other facilities. By the mid-1970s, school desegregation had become fact as well as law in more than 80 percent of all southern public schools (a better record than in the North, where residential segregation remains pronounced). The protection of the right to vote represents the civil rights movement's greatest success: When Congress passed the Voting Rights Act in 1965, barely 100 African Americans held elective office in the country; by 2000 there were more than 9,000.

Rosa Parks Refuses to Give Up Her Seat

Douglas Brinkley

The following selection, taken from a biography of Rosa Parks, traces the events of the late afternoon and evening of December 1, 1955, that sparked the Montgomery Bus Boycott. Thanks to decades-long laws and customs, African Americans were not permitted to sit in the middle sections of city buses if white customers needed those seats. But that day a forty-two-year-old seamstress and occasional activist refused to give up her seat. Rosa Parks was tired after a long day at work and, when challenged by a bus driver she had avoided for years because of a past confrontation, she simply said "no." Parks ended up being taken into custody by the Montgomery, Alabama, police, and news of the incident quickly reached family, friends, and acquaintances. Among them were figures, both black and white, connected with African American organizations and the civil rights movement. Douglas Brinkley is a Distinguished Professor of History at Rice University and a commentator for CBS News.

SOURCE. Douglas Brinkley, *Rosa Parks*. Houston: Lipper Viking, 2000, pp. 105–110, 112–115. Copyright © 2000 by Douglas Brinkley. All rights reserved. Used by permission of Viking Penguin, a division of Penguin Group (USA) Inc. and the author.

Shortly after 5:00 P.M., Rosa Parks clocked out of work and walked the block to Court Square to wait for her bus home. It had been a hard day, and her body ached, from her feet swollen from the constant standing to her shoulders throbbing from the strain and her chronic bursitis. But the bus stand was packed, so Parks, disinclined to jockey for a rush-hour seat, crossed Dexter Avenue to do a little shopping at Lee's Cut-Rate Drug. She had decided to treat herself to a heating pad but found them too pricey. Instead, she bought some Christmas gifts, along with aspirin, toothpaste, and a few other sundries, and headed back to the bus stop wondering how her husband's day had been at the Maxwell Air Force Base Barber Shop and thinking about what her mother would cook for dinner.

It was in this late-day reverie that Rosa Parks dropped her dime in the box and boarded the yellow-olive city bus. She took an aisle seat in the racially neutral middle section, behind the movable sign which read "colored." She was not expecting any problems, as there were several empty spaces at the whites-only front of the bus. A black man was sitting next to her on her right and staring out the window; across the aisle sat two black women deep in conversation. At the next two stops enough white passengers got on to nearly fill up the front section. At the third stop, in front of the Empire Theater, a famous shrine to country-music fans as the stage where the legendary Hank Williams got his start, the last front seats were taken, with one man left standing.

> The bus driver twisted around and locked his eyes on Rosa Parks.

Making Her Choice

The bus driver twisted around and locked his eyes on Rosa Parks. Her heart almost stopped when she saw it was James F. Blake, the bully who had put her off his bus twelve years earlier. She didn't know his name, but since that incident in 1943, she had never boarded a bus that Blake was driving. This day, however, she had absentmindedly stepped in. "Move y'all, I want those two seats," the driver barked on behalf of Jim Crow [laws segregating blacks and whites], which dictated that all four blacks in that row of the middle section would have to surrender their seats to accommodate the single white man, as no "colored" could be allowed to sit parallel with him. A stony silence fell over the bus as nobody moved. "Y'all better make it light on yourselves and let me have those seats," Blake sputtered, more impatiently than before. Quietly and in unison, the two black women sitting across from Parks rose and moved to the back. Her seatmate quickly followed suit, and she swung her legs to the side to let him out. Then Parks slid over to the window and gazed out at the Empire Theater marquee promoting *A Man Alone*, a new Western starring Ray Milland.

The next ten seconds seemed like an eternity to Rosa Parks. As Blake made his way toward her, all she could think about were her forebears, who, as [poet] Maya Angelou would put it, took the lash, the branding iron, and untold humiliations while only praying that their children would someday "flesh out" the dream of equality. But unlike the poet, it was not Africa in the days of the slave trade that Parks was thinking about; it was racist Alabama in the here and now. She shuddered with the memory of her grandfather back in Pine Level keeping watch for the KKK [Ku Klux Klan] every night with a loaded shotgun in his lap, echoing [pre–Civil War] abolitionist John Brown's exhortation: "Talk! Talk! Talk! That didn't free the slaves. . . . What is needed is action! Action!" So when Parks looked up at Blake, his hard, thoughtless scowl filled her with pity. She felt fearless, bold, and serene. "Are you going to stand up?" the driver demanded. Rosa Parks looked straight at him and said: "No." Flustered and not quite sure what to do, Blake retorted, "Well, I'm going to have you arrested." And Parks, still sitting next to the window, replied softly, "You may do that."

Her majestic use of "may" rather than "can" put Parks on the high ground, establishing her as a protester, not a victim. "When I made that decision," Parks stated later, "I knew I had the strength of my ancestors with me," and obviously their dignity as well. And her formal dignified "No," uttered on a suppertime bus in the cradle of the Confederacy as darkness fell, ignited the collective "no" of black history in America, a defiance as liberating as John Brown's on the gallows in Harpers Ferry [Virginia].

A Decisive Moment

The situation put Blake in a bind. This woman would, of course, have to be evicted from his bus. But should he do it himself, or should he call the police? Would it be better just to take her name and address and report her to the authorities later? Uncertain of what to do, he radioed his supervisor. "I see it said as how I got up and swore at her and then went and called the police and told them to come get her," Blake told *Washington Post* reporter Paul Hendrickson in 1989 after years of remaining silent about the incident. "Well, I called the company first, just like I was supposed to do. Nobody ever wrote that.

> 'I don't know, but the law is the law, and you're under arrest.'

I got my supervisor on the line. He said, 'Did you warn her, Jim?' I said, 'I warned her.' And he said, and I remember it just like I'm standing here, 'Well, then, Jim, you do it. You got to exercise your powers and put her off, hear?' And that's just what I did."

Within minutes, Montgomery police officers F.B. Day and D.W. Mixon arrived and listened to Blake's account of what had transpired. Parks just watched as the three white men conferred on her fate, and realized what it would be: She would be fingerprinted and put in jail. The other passengers, black and white alike, began getting off the bus quietly but nervously, some with the self-possession to ask for transfers, others too anxious in the volatile situation. The blacks who remained on the bus sat in stunned, silent recognition that this time the authorities had picked the wrong woman to mess with. "It was like a mosque inside," one passenger recalled. "You could have heard a pin drop. It's as if we were all praying to Allah."

> By the time her arrest was processed at Montgomery's city hall, Rosa Parks's spirit had hardened.

The two policemen then boarded the bus, less than thrilled at the prospect of arresting a prim, well-mannered, middle-aged woman on charges of violating the segregation code. When Officer Day asked Parks why she had refused to stand, she replied with a question that had no moral answer: "Why do you all push us around?" Day responded with a shrug and the only justification he could muster: "I don't know, but the law is the law, and you're under arrest." Then he picked up Parks's purse, Mixon gathered her shopping bags, and together they escorted her to their squad car. They did not handcuff Parks or mistreat her in any way. In fact, Parks saw them as two tired beat cops with no desire to waste their time and effort writing up reports for minor offenses.

Taken into Custody

At that point Parks was only in police custody, not officially arrested. For that a warrant would have to be sworn out and signed at city hall. On the way there Officer Day, more curious than angry, again asked Parks, "Why didn't you stand up when the driver spoke to you?" This time she said nothing. Calm had descended upon her; Parks had entrusted herself to the Lord's hands.

Just about everyone who hears the story of Rosa Parks asks the same question: Was her refusal to give

up her seat premeditated? Did she intend to become the NAACP's [National Association for the Advancement of Colored People] test case against segregation? The answer to both is no. Rosa Parks did not wake up on the morning of December 1, 1955, primed for a showdown over civil rights with the local police. A lifetime's education in injustice—from her grandfather's nightly vigils to the murder of Emmett Till [an African American teenager murdered for allegedly flirting with a white woman]—had strengthened her resolve to act when the time came. What arose in Parks that fateful evening was her belief in what Dr. Martin Luther King, Jr., often said: that "some of us must bear the burden of trying to save the soul of America." On her way home that night, Parks had no intention of making the headlines or history: She was thinking about relaxing for a rare moment, propping her feet up on the sofa, listening to a couple of Christmas carols, and preparing for that evening's NAACP Youth Council meeting. But when a white man tried to use an unfair system to undermine her dignity, Rosa Parks realized that it was *her burden* to stay put. "Just having paid for a seat and riding for only a couple blocks and then having to stand was too much," she told the Highlander Folk School's executive committee at a meeting a few months later. "These other persons had got on the bus after I did. It meant that I didn't have a right to do anything but get on the bus, give them my fare, and then be pushed wherever they wanted me. . . . There had to be a stopping place, and this seemed to have been the place for me to stop being pushed around and to find out what human rights I had, if any."

By the time her arrest was processed at Montgomery's city hall, Rosa Parks's spirit had hardened. She knew that the police were wrong, that she *had* sat in the "colored section," that she *had* obeyed the rules. Parched from the ordeal, she eyed a water fountain, and Officer Day gave her permission to take a drink. But Officer Mixon

Photo on previous page: Rosa Parks had just left her job as a seamstress when she boarded the bus that would lead to her arrest. (Don Cravens/ Contributor/Time & Life Pictures/Getty Images.)

quickly stepped in. "No! You can't drink no water," he shouted. "It's for whites only. You have to wait till you get to the jail." It was the only time that Parks grew angry during her arrest—a grown man, a law enforcement officer no less, and presumably a Christian, was denying a tired, middle-aged woman a sip of water. She couldn't help but think of the Roman soldiers who had given Jesus only vinegar to drink on the road to Calvary.

Parks filled out the required forms and asked if she could make a telephone call to let her husband know where she was. Her request was denied. As the policemen escorted her from city hall to their squad car, she remembers chuckling to herself. Who would have thought that little Rosa McCauley [her maiden name]—whose friends teased her for being such a Goody Two-shoes in her dainty white gloves—would ever become a convicted criminal, much less a subversive worthy of police apprehension, in the eyes of the state of Alabama? . . .

> Word of Rosa Parks's arrest had already spread through Montgomery's black community.

Starting a Movement

After another hour or so, Parks was allowed to telephone home. Her mother answered. "I'm in jail," her daughter stated matter-of-factly. "See if Parks will come down here and get me out." Raymond Parks was on the line in a flash to make sure his wife was okay. She reassured him that the police were cordial and that she had not been beaten. "I'll be there in a few minutes," he told her, but she knew it would be longer than that, as they didn't own a car. "My husband was very upset," Parks recalled. "My mother was, too. After they found that I was okay—that I hadn't been physically manhandled—they felt better."

Word of Rosa Parks's arrest had already spread through Montgomery's black community. Another passenger on the bus that would go down in history had told Parks's friend Bertha Butler about the showdown with Blake. Butler had immediately contacted E.D. Nixon's wife, Arlet, with the shocking news that angelic Rosa Parks had been arrested. Arlet Nixon left a message for her husband at his office downtown, then paced around their Clinton Avenue home wondering what to do. She was relieved when he finally rang back, asking, "What's up?"

"You won't believe it," Arlet Nixon replied. "The police got Rosa. She's in jail, but nobody knows the extent of the charges or whether she's been beaten. You better get her out." All Nixon could manage in response was, "Holy mother of God." He called the police station to find out what the charges were, but "they wouldn't talk with me because I was black," he remembered. "They couldn't have been ruder." So Nixon decided to seek the help of his friend Clifford Durr, a white lawyer the police would have to cooperate with.

"I asked Clifford if he would call the jail and find out why in hell they arrested Rosa Parks," Nixon recalled. Durr did so immediately, especially outraged that a friend was being denied her civil liberties. The officer he talked to told Durr that Rosa Parks had been booked for violating the city's segregation ordinance, with bail set at one hundred dollars. Their paying white clients having abandoned them, the Durrs were broke, so Nixon offered to post Parks's bond himself. But even so, he asked Durr to come to the jail with him for fear that corrupt police would try to take his money without releasing Parks. The Durrs found themselves heading to the city jail in E.D. Nixon's blue Plymouth to bail out their friend, all discussing the possibility of making this the NAACP's Jim Crow test case. They all agreed that the moment for action had arrived. "I waited for them while they made bail," Virginia Durr wrote later in *Outside the Magic Circle*. "Everything went very smoothly. They brought

Mrs. Parks out from behind the bars. That was a terrible sight to see: this gentle, lovely, sweet woman, whom I knew and was so fond of, being brought down by a matron. She wasn't in handcuffs, but they had to unlock two or three doors that grated loudly."

What impressed Virginia Durr most about the moment was how tranquil Rosa Parks remained, the epitome of grace under pressure. As Nixon signed the bond papers, Raymond Parks came in, close to tears. He gave his wife a hear hug that swept her off her feet as her two-hour ordeal came to an end. The Durrs hopped into Nixon's Plymouth, and the trio followed Raymond Parks, driving a car hastily borrowed from a friend, back to Cleveland Courts. There they held a powwow over coffee to take stock of what had happened.

Nixon refrained from discussing legal strategies straight off, sensing that Rosa Parks wanted to return to normalcy—to change her clothes, eat dinner, and run her regular Thursday NAACP Youth Council meeting at the tiny Trinity Lutheran Church across the street. When Nixon accompanied her to the church, however, he used their rime alone to lobby his friend to let her arrest become a civil-rights test case, taking care not to push too hard and to give Parks time to assess her options. This was not easy, for from the moment he had first heard A. Philip Randolph speak of civil rights in St. Louis, E. D. Nixon had been itching for a direct confrontation with "Mr. Charlie," as he called the white power establishment. He couldn't help but see it as a gift from God that Mr. Charlie had been fool enough to arrest Rosa Parks, but to his consternation, he sensed reluctance on the part of his intended heroine. Nixon asserted in an interview that he had to prod Parks into faking a public stand, a contention strongly disputed by Virginia Foster Durr. "Mr. Nixon remembers her as being extremely reluctant to do it, but I remember that it was her husband who was so reluctant," Durr recalled. "He kept saying, over and over again: 'Rosa, the white folks will kill you. Rosa, the white folks will kill you.' It was like a background chorus—to hear the poor man, who was as white as he could be himself—for a black man, saying, 'Rosa, the white folks will kill you.' I don't remember her being reluctant."

But Rosa Parks would not be rushed into a decision; she had to consider the potential impact of filing a lawsuit on her husband and mother, both of whom were aghast at the prospect of Rosa's becoming a public spectacle. For one thing, she was the family's principal breadwinner, and becoming the NAACP poster woman for desegregation was bound to get her fired from her job at Montgomery Fair. What's more, Parks's husband and mother had been warning her for years that working with E. D. Nixon and the NAACP would get her lynched from the tallest telephone pole in town someday. It was one thing to be arrested for an isolated bus incident; it was quite another, as historian Taylor Branch would put it in *Parting the Waters*, to "reenter that forbidden zone by choice."

> In her heart [Rosa Parks] never doubted what she had to do.

Rosa Parks already knew, of course, that a court case would turn her into even more of an outcast in white Montgomery. Although unconcerned about her own physical safety, she also knew that any public position she took would cause dire trouble for her husband: the police would harass him, perhaps even frame him on some trumped-up charge. Her mother's health, meanwhile, was frail: Could she endure a long-drawn-out trial? Rosa Parks fretted over these dilemmas, but in her heart she never doubted what she had to do.

Montgomery's Activists State Their Grievances

Citizen's Mass Meeting

The Montgomery Bus Boycott began on December 5, 1955, four days after Rosa Parks's arrest for refusing to give up her seat to a white man. The boycott was called for by civil rights leaders such as E.D. Dixon of the National Association for the Advancement of Colored People (NAACP) and Jo Ann Robinson of the Women's Political Council, but it turned into a major effort enjoying mass support when, the evening of December 13, huge crowds met at Montgomery's Holt Street Baptist Church. There, ministers such as Ralph David Abernathy and Montgomery newcomer Martin Luther King Jr. added their voices to support the boycott and a legal challenge designed to end segregation on the city's privately-owned buses. The following selection is the resolution taken by those who met that evening. The resolution, soon printed in the area's principal African American newspaper, served as the first major public statement of the boycott's purpose.

Photo on following page: Rev. Martin Luther King Jr. speaks to an overflow crowd at a mass meeting at the Holt Street Baptist Church during the bus boycott. (Gene Herrick/ Associated Press.)

SOURCE. Darlene Clark Hine, "Chapter 3 Overview: Fighting Back," The Eyes on the Prize: Civil Rights Reader, Clayborne Carson, et. al. New York, NY: Viking, 1991, pp. 54–56. Copyright © 1987, 1991 by Blackside, Inc. All rights reserved. Used by permission of Viking Penguin, a division of Penguin Group (USA) Inc..

WHEREAS, there are thousands of Negroes in the city and county of Montgomery who ride busses owned and operated by the Montgomery City Lines, Incorporated, and

WHEREAS, said citizens have been riding busses owned and operated by said company over a number of years, and

WHEREAS, said citizens, over a number of years, and on many occasions have been insulted, embarrassed and have been made to suffer great fear of bodily harm by drivers of busses owned and operated by said bus company, and

WHEREAS, the drivers of said busses have never requested a white passenger riding on any of its busses to relinquish his seat and stand so that a Negro may take his seat; however, said drivers have on many occasions too numerous to mention requested Negro passengers on said busses to relinquish their seats and stand so that white passengers may take their seats, and

WHEREAS, said citizens of Montgomery city and county pay their fares just as all other persons who are passengers on said busses, and are entitled to fair and equal treatment, and

WHEREAS, there has been any number of arrests of Negroes caused by drivers of said busses and they are constantly put in jail for refusing to give white passengers their seats and stand.

WHEREAS, in March of 1955, a committee of citizens did have a conference with one of the officials of said bus line; at which time said official arranged a meeting between attorneys representing the Negro citizens of this city and attorneys representing the Montgomery City Lines, Incorporated and the city of Montgomery, and

WHEREAS, the official of the bus line promised that as a result of the meeting between said attorneys, he would issue a statement of policy clarifying the law with reference to the seating of Negro passengers on the bus, and

WHEREAS, said attorneys did have a meeting and did discuss the matter of clarifying the law, however, the official said bus lines did not make public statements as to its policy with reference to the seating of passengers on its busses, and

> Citizens of Montgomery city and county believe that they have been grossly mistreated as passengers on the busses.

WHEREAS, since that time, at least two ladies have been arrested for an alleged violation of the city segregation law with reference to bus travel, and

WHEREAS, said citizens of Montgomery city and county believe that they have been grossly mistreated as passengers on the busses owned and operated by said bus company in spite of the fact that they are in the majority with reference to the number of passengers riding on said busses.

Be It Resolved As Follows:

1. That the citizens of Montgomery are requesting that every citizen in Montgomery, regardless of race, color or creed, to refrain from riding busses owned and operated in the city of Montgomery by the Montgomery City Lines, Incorporated until some arrangement has been worked out between said citizens and the Montgomery City Lines, Incorporated.

2. That every person owning or who has access to automobiles use their automobiles in assisting other persons to get to work without charge.

3. That the employers of persons whose employees live a . . . distance from them, as much as possible afford transportation to your own employees.

4. That the Negro citizens of Montgomery are ready and willing to send a delegation of citizens to the Montgomery City Lines to discuss their grievances and to work out a solution for the same.

Be it further resolved that we have not, are not, and have no intentions of using an unlawful means or any intimidation to persuade persons not to ride the Montgomery City Lines' busses. However, we call upon your consciences, both moral and spiritual, to give your whole-hearted support to this undertaking. We believe we have [a just] complaint and we are willing to discuss this matter with the proper officials.

White People Had Varied Reactions to the Montgomery Bus Boycott

David Halberstam

The following selection examines how white leaders in Montgomery, Alabama, responded to the boycott, as well as some of the ways in which it turned into an event of national significance. Many white leaders, in the first weeks of the boycott, believed that it would not hold. But they quickly learned that not only were the protesters sincere and determined, their nonviolent, dignified approach was drawing respect from both inside and outside Montgomery. Local newspaper and television coverage, which was often carried out by younger journalists sympathetic to civil rights, soon reached a broader, national audience. Meanwhile, the boycott's leaders

SOURCE. David Halberstam, *The Fifties*. New York: Villard Books, 1993, pp. 555–557, 559–562. Copyright © 1993 by The Amateurs Limited. All rights reserved. Reproduced by permission of Random House, Inc.

grew more sophisticated in their understanding of this publicity. Notable among them was Martin Luther King Jr., whom the author argues was at least partially made famous by Montgomery whites trying to turn him into a villain. David Halberstam was a Pulitzer Prize–winning author and journalist. Among his many books are *The Best and the Brightest*, a key study of the Vietnam War, and *The Next Century*.

The white community had no idea how to deal with the boycott. The city leadership thought it was dealing with the black leadership from the past—poorly educated, readily divided, lacking endurance, and without access to national publicity outlets. When the boycott proved to be remarkably successful on the first day, the mayor of Montgomery, W.A. Gayle, did not sense that something historic was taking place, nor did he move to accommodate the blacks, who were in fact not asking for integrated buses but merely a minimal level of courtesy and a fixed line between the sections. Gayle turned to a friend and said, "Comes the first rainy day and the Negroes will be back on the buses." Soon it did rain, but the boycott continued. As the movement grew stronger, the principal response of Gayle and his two commissioners was to join the White Citizens' Council [a racist group]. A month after the boycott began, it proved so successful that the bus-line operators were asking for permission to double the price from ten to twenty cents a ride. They were granted a five-cent raise. In late January, frustrated by the solidarity of the blacks, the white leadership went to three relatively obscure black ministers and tricked them into saying, or at least seeming to say, that they accepted the city's terms and would show up at a meeting at city hall. Then

> 'Comes the first rainy day and the Negroes will be back on the buses.'

WHERE DID JIM CROW LAWS SEGREGATE TRANSPORTATION?

Taken from: Educational Broadcasting Corp. www.pbs.org.

the *Montgomery Advertiser* was brought in—a disgraceful moment for a newspaper—to report on the alleged agreement and make it seem, without using the names of the three ministers, that the real black leadership had conceded. By chance the real black leadership found out, and the ploy was not successful. But it was a sign of how terrified and out of touch the white leadership was—as if it could, by means of disinformation, halt a movement as powerful as this. When the hoax was discovered, the mayor was petulant. No more Mr. Nice Guy, he threatened. "No other city in the South of our size has treated the Negroes more fairly," he said. Now he wanted his fellow whites to be made of sterner stuff and to stop helping their maids and workers to get to work by giving them transportation money and, worse, giving them rides. "The Negroes," he said, "are laughing at white people behind their backs. They think it is funny and amusing that whites who are opposed to the Negro boycott will act as chauffeurs to Negroes who are boycotting the buses."

Reaction and Outside Support

The Montgomery authorities stopped the local black cabdrivers from ferrying people to and from work in groups of five and six for ten cents a ride (there was an old city ordinance that said the minimum fare for a ride had to be 45 cents), but money poured in from the outside to buy some fifteen new station wagons. Eventually, the MIA [Montgomery Improvement Association] had some thirty cars of its own. Richard Harris, a local black pharmacist who was a crucial dispatcher in the downtown area, feared that his phone was tapped, so he spoke in comic black dialect to confuse the white authorities, and he used a code with other dispatchers—"shootin' marbles," for example, told how many people needed to be picked up.

Inevitably, the city leaders resorted to what had always worked in the past: the use of police power. The city fathers decided that it had to break the back of the carpool, and soon the police started arresting carpool drivers. On January 26, 1956, some eight weeks into the boycott, Martin Luther King, Jr., was arrested for driving 30 miles an hour in a 25-mile-an-hour zone. He was taken to the police station and fingerprinted; at first it appeared that he would be kept overnight, but because the crowd of blacks outside the station kept growing larger and noisier, the police let King go on his own recognizance. Two days later, King's house was bombed by a white extremist, the first in a series of such incidents at the homes of black leaders and at black churches.

In unity and nonviolence the blacks found new strength, particularly as the nation began to take notice.

> In unity and nonviolence the blacks found new strength.

Things that had for so long terrified them—the idea of being arrested and spending the night in prison, for example—became a badge of honor. Their purpose now was greater than their terror. More, because the nation was watching, the jails were becoming safer. King was, in effect, taking a crash course in the uses of modern media and proving a fast learner. Montgomery was becoming a big story, and the longer it went on, the bigger it became. In the past it had been within the power of such papers as the *Advertiser* and its afternoon twin, the far more racist *Alabama Journal*, either to grant or not grant coverage to black protests and to slant the coverage in terms most satisfying to the whites. The power to deny coverage was a particularly important aspect of white authority, for if coverage was denied, the blacks would feel isolated and gradually lose heart (for taking such risks without anyone knowing or caring); in addition, the whites would be able to crush any protest with far fewer witnesses and far less scrutiny. But that power deserted the local newspapers now, in no small part because the Montgomery story was too important for even the most virulently segregationist newspaper to ignore completely, affecting as it did virtually every home in the city; second, because even when the local newspapers tried to control the coverage, and at the very least minimize it, the arrival of television meant that the newspapers were no longer the only potential journalistic witnesses. . . .

Sympathetic Media Coverage

But even though the two Montgomery papers were owned by the same company, they no longer had a monopoly on news. Just a year earlier, on Christmas Day 1954, WSFA-TV had gone on the air. There had been one other local channel, but it did no local programming. From the start, it was announced, there would be active local news and weather coverage—fifteen minutes of news, and fifteen minutes of weather each

Dr. Martin Luther King Jr.

The person most closely associated with the civil rights movement of the 1950s and 1960s was a Baptist minister named Martin Luther King Jr. Indeed, King's fame is so great that he is an icon of American history with a national holiday maintained in his honor. But until the Montgomery Bus Boycott made him a national figure, King was little known except as a young minister newly called to Montgomery, Alabama, in 1955.

Martin Luther King Jr. was born in Atlanta, Georgia, in 1929. His father was a Baptist minister as well. Although the younger King had early doubts about Christianity, he went on to earn a degree in divinity from Crozer Theological Seminary in Pennsylvania in 1951, after having already earned a bachelor's degree from Morehouse College in Atlanta. He became a doctor of theology with a PhD from Boston University in 1955. By then, he had already settled, along with his wife, Coretta Scott, in Montgomery, and he had taken up a position at the Dexter Avenue Baptist Church.

Ministers often played large roles in African American communities, and the young King was no exception. He quickly became acquainted with such activists as E.D. Dixon and served on numerous community boards and associations. When the bus boycott began, King

evening, something almost unheard of locally in those days. Indeed, there was said to be a hot new news director arriving from Oklahoma City. The news director (and star reporter as well, of course) was a young man named Frank McGee, then in his early thirties. He was, in fact, a very good reporter, and he immediately decided that the bus boycott was a very big story. Unlike his local print counterparts, he did not take the protest as a social affront. Rather, he realized it was the kind of high drama that lent itself exceptionally well to television. Nor was McGee, like his counterparts at the two Montgomery papers, part of the town's white power establishment. He had grown up very poor in northern Louisiana and then in Oklahoma, and he sympathized with all poor people, white and black. He liked to joke emerged as the head of the Montgomery Improvement Association and, despite attacks on his own house and family (which resulted in no injuries), he insisted that the protest remain peaceful. His position on nonviolence was formed during his theological studies, which had introduced him to such proponents of nonviolent resistance as Mohandas Gandhi. For the rest of his career, King continued to preach nonviolence despite arrests, fines, and even jail terms.

Following the success of the Montgomery boycott, King formed the Southern Christian Leadership Conference, a key civil rights organization with national reach. Over the next years King and the organization led or participated in protests, marches, and other movements in favor of desegregation, social equality, and labor rights. King himself was, by the early 1960s, a familiar figure in American life and even internationally as the winner of the 1963 Nobel Peace Prize. King's leadership is credited as being one of the factors behind the passage of the broad Civil Rights Act of 1964.

On April 4, 1968, Martin Luther King Jr. was assassinated in Memphis, Tennessee, where he had gone to support a local black workers' association. President Lyndon B. Johnson proclaimed a national day of mourning in his honor.

that his father, who worked the oil rigs, might have risen up out of some back country swamp, "and you never know what color there might be in our family if you went back far enough." In an age when most of the nation's top journalists seemed to be the product of the nation's elite schools, Frank McGee had never gone to college and had a high school degree only because he finished a high-school equivalency course while in the service. He was not a particularly ideological man, but like most reporters of that era, he sympathized instinctively with the blacks, whose demands were so rudimentary. He was well aware of the dangers of covering the story, that the television journalists were vulnerable to attack. But although there were constant threats, both in the streets and over the phone, no one ever assaulted him. What surprised him most, he later would say, was that the local station managers never cramped his style, never told him what he could and could not put on the air. Part of the reason, he suspected, was that his bosses thought they needed all the excitement they could get in those early days in order to compete with the local newspapers. Besides, his bosses were too new to be part of the establishment.

The Boycott Reaches TV

Like many of his generation, he was aware that he was riding a very good story. That was particularly true as the whites blindly continued to resist and the story continued to escalate. The NBC network news show, also still in its infancy, started to use McGee with increasing regularity on the network, with a direct feed from Montgomery. It was not only a good story, in which ordinary Americans were asserting their demands for the most basic rights, but it was also helping McGee's career, which for a young, tough-minded, ambitious reporter was almost an unbeatable combination. (Within a year of the bus settlement, Frank McGee became one of NBC's first national network correspondents.) Events were soon beyond the ability of the *Advertiser* to control coverage. Montgomery was soon flooded with members of the national press, causing [Montgomery newspaper editor] Grover Hall to comment that he was "duenna [chaperone] and Indian guide to more than a hundred reporters of the international press." The more coverage there was, the more witnesses there were and the harder it was for the white leadership to inflict physical violence upon the blacks. In addition, the more coverage there was, the more it gave courage to the leadership and its followers. The sacrifices and the risks were worth it, everyone sensed, because the country and the world were now taking notice. What was at stake in the *Advertiser*'s coverage of Martin King and the Montgomery bus boycott was, the editors of that paper soon learned to their surprise, not King's reputation but the *Advertiser*'s reputation.

The national press corps that had coalesced for the first time at the Emmett Till trial [of the accused white murderers of a fourteen-year-old black boy] only a few months earlier returned in full strength, and its sympathies were not with Mayor Gayle, who appointed a committee to meet with the black ministers and added a White Citizens' Council member to it, or with police commissioner Clyde Sellers, who publicly joined the Citizens' Council in the middle of the struggle, saying, "I wouldn't trade my Southern birthright for 100 Negro votes." Rather, the national reporters were impressed with the dignity of Rosa Parks, the seriousness of the young Martin King, and the shrewd charm of Ralph Abernathy.

> Ironically, it was the white leaders of Montgomery who first helped to create the singular importance of Martin King.

The Role of Martin Luther King Jr.

Ironically, it was the white leaders of Montgomery who first helped to create the singular importance of Martin King. Convinced that ordinary black people were being tricked and manipulated, they needed a villain. If they could weaken, discredit, or scare him, then their problems would be solved, they thought. Gradually, he became the focal point of the boycott. "I have the feeling," Bayard Rustin, the nation's most experienced civil rights organizer, told him at the time, "that the Lord has laid his hands on you, and that is a dangerous, dangerous thing." Still, King had no illusions about his role: "If Martin Luther King had never been born this movement would have taken place," he said early on. "I just happened to be there. You know there comes a time when time itself is ready for a change. That time has come in Montgomery and I have nothing to do with it."

For a time the role was almost too much for him. The amount of hate mail was staggering, and it was filled with threats that he had to take seriously. His father pleaded with him to leave Montgomery and return to Atlanta. "It's better to be a live dog than a dead lion," Daddy King said. The pressure on King was such that he was getting little sleep, and he was truly afraid. He realized for the first time how sheltered his existence had been, how ill prepared he was to deal with the racial violence that was waiting just beneath the surface in the South. One night, unsure of whether to continue, he thought of all his religious training and he heard the voice of Christ: "Martin Luther, stand up for righteousness. Stand up for justice. Stand up for truth' . . . the fatigue had turned into hope." . . .

The boycott continued. The white leadership was paralyzed; in late February, it cited an obscure state law prohibiting boycotts and indicted eighty-nine leaders, including twenty-four ministers and all the drivers of the carpools. The real target, however, was King. He happened to be in Nashville lecturing when the indictments were announced. Back in Montgomery, many of the other leaders were giving themselves up in groups to show their defiance. King flew back to Montgomery by way of Atlanta. In Atlanta, his father pleaded with him not to go back. "They gon' to kill my boy," he told the Atlanta police chief. He brought over some of Martin's oldest friends, including Benjamin Mays, the president of Morehouse [the college in Atlanta King attended], to help talk him out of returning. But Martin Luther King, Jr., was firm now. Not to return, to desert his friends at this point, would be the height of cowardice, he told them. "I have begun the struggle," he said, "and I can't turn back. I have reached the point of no return." At that point his father broke down and began to sob. Benjamin Mays told him he was doing the right thing, and he returned to Montgomery.

Photo on opposite page: Black citizens of Montgomery faced intimidation by white supremacists during the bus boycott. (**Associated Press**.)

Rosa Parks's Example Traveled Across the Atlantic to Great Britain

Robert Verkaik

In the following selection, a British journalist examines how a young black man, Paul Stephenson, used the example of Rosa Parks to challenge the discrimination that existed in Britain until the mid-1960s. Stephenson did so by starting a bus boycott in the English city of Bristol in 1963. The boycott lasted for sixty days, attracting the attention and support of activists and government officials. Eventually, the company that managed Bristol's buses agreed to hire blacks as drivers and conductors. The Bristol Bus Boycott was a major strike against Britain's "colour bar," which legalized discrimination in hiring and the denial of other rights to Britain's growing populations of blacks and Asians, many of whom were recent immigrants from the nation's former colonies in Africa, the West Indies, Pakistan, and India. According to the author—who finishes his report with comments from observers on Britain's current racial concerns—Stephenson credits Rosa Parks with beginning a movement that, in 1965, led to the lifting of the color bar in the UK. Robert Verkaik is a British journalist and editor whose work appears in the *Independent* and the *Daily Mail*.

It was the defining moment in Britain's black civil rights movement that finally forced the Government to tackle racism in society.

Paul Stephenson, a young black teacher from Bristol [England], led a victorious boycott against a racist bus company in 1963 that paved the way for the country's first race laws 40 years ago. His stand earned him comparisons with Rosa Parks, the woman who inspired the civil rights movement of America by her refusal to give up her seat on a bus to a white man in segregated Alabama in 1955.

In an exclusive interview with *The Independent*, Mr. Stephenson said he was directly inspired by Ms. Parks' own protest eight years earlier: "You couldn't help but be impressed by Martin Luther King and what he was doing in America. But without Rosa Parks I'm not sure whether we would have embarked on our boycott. She was a huge influence on me. I thought if she could protest by not giving up her seat on a bus we could start a bus boycott."

The Bristol bus company had enforced a strict colour bar by refusing to employ blacks or Asians. The company claimed white women would refuse to ride on buses driven by black men or would feel unsafe if they employed black bus conductors. It was an act of blatant racism and provoked Mr. Stephenson, then a 26-year-old teacher and community officer working in St. Pauls in Bristol, to lead a 60-day boycott of the city's buses.

His protest was supported by thousands of local people who shunned the buses to show their disgust for

Photo on following page: Trevor Phillips, head of the British Commission for Racial Equality, addresses the media to discuss bigotry in the police force. (Graeme Robertson/Staff/Getty Images.)

the treatment of ethic minorities in the city. News of the protest quickly spread beyond Bristol.

On 28 August the company finally capitulated and agreed to lift the bar. It was the same day that Martin Luther King delivered his "I have a dream" speech.

News of the "bus boycott" spread and Mr. Stephenson was invited to Virginia by some of the black civil rights leaders of America.

The Labour [British political party] MP [member of Parliament] Tony Benn and West Indian cricketer Learie Constantine, later Lord Constantine, came to Bristol to join the protest. Harold Wilson, then the leader of the opposition, wrote to Mr. Stephenson offering his encouragement.

Mr. Stephenson, whose grandmother was a famous Victorian actress, was born in Rochford, Essex, and lived his early years in almost exclusively white communities. "I was treated [as] more of a novelty than anything else because most black and Asian people tended to live in the cities."

Mr. Stephenson later became a cause celebre in his own right when he refused to leave a Bristol pub until he was served half a pint of bitter. When he stood trial on a charge of failing to leave a licensed premises his case attracted national publicity. *The Daily Express* put the story on the front page and entitled it "The man who refused to say please for his beer".

The Bristol bus boycott and Mr. Stephenson's own case helped to thrust race into the national limelight and change public opinion about the treatment of blacks and Asians living in Britain. Few doubt that without Mr. Stephenson's efforts it would have been difficult for [UK prime minister] Harold Wilson's Labour government to bring in Britain's first anti-discrimination laws.

Mr. [Trevor] Phillips [head of the Commission for Racial Equality (CRE)] said: "Everybody forgets that the 1965 law came about because bus companies would not employ black conductors and drivers because white passengers, particularly women, complained they could not get on a bus with a black conductor. At the time it was perfectly reasonable for a bus company to give that as a reason for not employing someone black. Paul Stephenson led a boycott and people don't give him enough credit for his actions." For the CRE, the issue of Britian's attitude towards race relations is still critical. Mr. Phillips himself has tried to reset the race agenda by warning that the country is "sleepwalking into segregation".

> While treatment of ethnic minorities in Britain has greatly improved in the past 40 years, the issue of race has not gone away.

Mr. Stephenson, who is married and still lives in Bristol, has continued his work on race issues.

He says that while treatment of ethnic minorities in Britain has greatly improved in the past 40 years, the issue of race has not gone away.

How Much Progress Has Been Made?

Lee Jasper, Secretary of the National Assembly Against Racism: "In the last 40 years we made slow progress in tackling racism. . . . The Government plans to abolish the Commission for Racial Equality and replace it with a single Commission on Equalities and Human Rights. Any progress made in the last 40 years and any hope of delivering racial equality in my or my children's lifetime will be lost."

Sadiq Khan, Labour MP for Tooting [London]: "When my father came to this country from Pakistan in the 1960s, there were signs up saying: 'No blacks, no Irish, no dogs.' That attitude led to clusters of various ethnicities living together because of safety in numbers, which is worth remembering when people start lecturing the ethnic minorities about segregation. In the last 40 years the situation has improved."

Diane Abbot, Labour MP for Hackney North and Stoke Newington [London]: "My parents were brought up in rural Jamaica, left school at 14 and came to Britain in the early 1950s. They lived to see their daughter become a British Member of Parliament. That is a measure of how far we have come. And it is remarkable, not that there are tensions, but how well ethnic minorities do manage to get along."

Trevor Phillips, Chairman of the Commission for Racial Equality: "We are now moving into the territory where patterns of racial bias are emerging in spite of everybody doing the right thing. We have to address this more sensibly and address the real issues. The first thing is to recognise that there's a physical basis for separation but that doesn't mean people never have to meet each other."

The Legacy of Rosa Parks Is Clear in Contemporary Montgomery

Nancy Snow

December 1 remains a day to commemorate Rosa Parks, the author of the following selection suggests. Published on the fifty-fifth anniversary of the day Parks refused to give up her bus seat to a white man, the selection makes the argument that the day marked a key moment in the history of the civil rights movement in the United States. The author makes clear that the city that once tried to deny Rosa Parks the basic privilege of equal rights now offers many monuments to her. As such, it is a signal of the changes that one person can inspire. Nancy Snow is professor of communications at California State University, Fullerton, and the author of six books, including *Persuader in Chief: Global Opinion and Public Diplomacy in the Age of Obama*.

SOURCE. Nancy Snow, "Remembering Rosa Parks," *Huffington Post*, December 1, 2010. All rights reserved. Reproduced by permission of the author.

Two weeks ago today [December 1, 2010] I was in Montgomery, Alabama. Montgomery is called the Capital City of the American South, home to the short-lived Confederate presidency of Jefferson Davis [and the] birthplace of the Civil Rights Movement. Its motto: Change happens here.

The sky was a typical Alabama bright blue, the weather sunny and crisp for a late November day. I drove downtown and there it was. A small commemorative sign dedicated to mark the spot where Rosa Parks refused to move to the back of the city bus. This was not far from the Montgomery Biscuits Class AA affiliate of the Tampa Bay Rays and the Renaissance Montgomery Hotel and Spa at the Convention Center. Change happens here.

Fifty-five years ago today, Mrs. Parks, the secretary of the local chapter of the National Association for the Advancement of Colored People, seared her legacy. She was not the first to refuse to take the designated "coloreds only" seat in the back. Many others had done so by December 1, 1955. Maybe it was her quiet resolve or the police mug shot of the middle-aged seamstress that led to a 381-day Montgomery bus boycott and a civil rights movement that found its spark.

Parks boarded a bus being driven by James Fred Blake. She had a long history with Blake. In 1943, he had ordered her off his bus for taking her seat from the front. Blacks were supposed to pay the driver from the front but then step out and board the bus from the back. That night Rosa Parks walked home in the rain after Blake drove off. Parks later said that she generally avoided Blake whenever she could. But on that December night in 1955, Parks had refused to move from the middle section of the bus and Blake called the police for her arrest. Blake explained: "I wasn't trying to do anything to that Parks woman except do my job. She was in violation of the city codes, so what was I supposed to do? That damn

The bus boycott and other protests during the civil rights movement culminated in the Civil Rights Act, signed into law by President Lyndon Johnson in 1964. (Associated Press.)

bus was full and she wouldn't move back. I had my orders." Blake remained a driver for the Montgomery city bus lines until 1974.

The Montgomery of Today

The Montgomery of today is a virtual shrine to her memory. There is Rosa L. Parks Avenue and Rosa Parks Place, a Rosa Parks branch of the Montgomery Library, the Rosa L. Parks city park, the Rosa Parks Quick Stop convenience store, Rosa Parks Place apartments and the Rosa L. Parks Avenue Church of God. Troy University sponsors the Rosa Parks Library and Museum. Ironically,

The Civil Rights Act of 1964

The civil rights movement that featured such protests as the Montgomery Bus Boycott culminated in the Civil Rights Act of 1964. The act guaranteed equal treatment under the law for both members of minority groups and women, and it provided a foundation for future civil rights measures. It also marked more subtle changes in the nature of the civil rights movement itself and even in the political makeup of the United States.

The act was signed into law by President Lyndon B. Johnson on July 2, 1964, after lengthy debate in Congress, and following extensive news coverage of the brutal murder of three civil rights workers in Mississippi. Such a measure had been originally proposed by Johnson's predecessor, John F. Kennedy, who was assassinated in 1963. Johnson, as the new president, believed that the passage of a broad civil rights measure would be a fine monument to Kennedy and set to work to get Congress to approve it. While some southern senators tried to filibuster the measure, or even to add "poison pills" (language or addenda intended to get people to vote against it), Johnson's persistence paid off. Among the major features of the act were portions forbidding state and local governments from denying access to public facilities on the basis of race, religion, gender, or ethnicity, as well as similar prohibitions directed at most employers. It also expanded the government's ability to act to guarantee equality under the law through such means as the Civil Rights Commission.

Rosa Parks the person left Montgomery, Alabama for Detroit, Michigan just two years after her history-making turn in that city bus. Her celebrity had led to threats. But the Rosa Parks legacy of conscientious objection continues.

Rosa Parks died in 2005 at the age of 92. She outlived Martin Luther King, Jr. by thirty-seven years. King was a 26-year-old minister at Dexter Avenue Baptist Church in Montgomery when the 42-year-old seamstress holding a bag of groceries refused to give up her seat to a white male passenger on the Cleveland Avenue bus line. Dr. King would become the spokesperson for the Bus Boycott and educate the people in the methods of nonviolent civil disobedience.

This "Mother of the Civil Rights Movement" was born in Tuskegee, Alabama, forty miles east of Montgomery, in a family whose heritage was African-American, Cherokee-Creek, and Scots-Irish. . . .

Many will celebrate the memory of Rosa Parks today. I think Google got it right [in an animated graphic used on Rosa Parks's birthday] with the image of children pouring out of a bus fifty-five years after Rosa Parks refused to move. It is idealistic, of course, but inspiring. The Civil Rights Movement continues to remind us of what one individual can do to create change. It happens here.

CHAPTER 2

Controversies Connected to the Montgomery Bus Boycott

Rosa Parks Changed the World

Ellen Goodman

According to the author of the following selection, Rosa Parks changed the world by not only her simple willingness to say "no" but also by setting an example. The author argues, in this piece written upon the death of Rosa Parks in 2005, that it is a mistake to believe that Parks was quiet and unassuming, as some commentators have. Instead, she was brave enough to challenge the accepted standards and norms of her time and culture. Beyond her importance as a key figure in the civil rights movement, Rosa Parks is an example of leadership in an environment that requires women, paradoxically, to be both brave and unassuming. Ellen Goodman is a writer whose work has appeared in more than three hundred newspapers, and she has also appeared frequently on television and radio. She is the author or co-author of eight books.

Photo on previous page: Police officers in Montgomery were accused of targeting black drivers for tickets during the bus boycott. (**Don Cravens/ Contributor/Time & Life Pictures/Getty Images.**)

It is remarkable how often the legend survives the legendary figure. So it is with Rosa Parks.

The mythology describes the woman who died Monday at 92 as a "humble seamstress." The textbooks pay homage to a "simple woman" with tired feet whose refusal to give up her seat on the bus to a white man half a century ago sparked a movement. The eulogies cast her as the "mother of the civil rights movement," as if it were an unplanned parenthood.

But the obituaries also suggest another side to her story. The "humble seamstress" was a civil rights activist long before that fateful bus ride. The "simple woman," secretary of her NAACP [National Association for the Advancement of Colored People] chapter, attended a leadership conference the summer before her act of civil disobedience. As for those tired feet? Parks herself wrote, "The only tired I was, was tired of giving in."

Is it possible we prefer our heroes to be humble? Or is it just our heroines? In her lifetime, Rosa Parks was often left off the dais of civil rights "leaders." In her death, she is lauded more as icon than as leader.

[Minister and civil rights figure] Al Sharpton, of all the un-humble politicians, praised Rosa Parks as someone who "changed American life, having never held public office, having no political ambition, just her quiet dignity and courage." Is this how we praise women? As unambitious, accidental heroines?

Women and Leadership

The subject of women and leadership is in the air, not just *on* the air. I heard of Parks's death here at a gathering of the Atlanta Women's Foundation, which is partnering with the White House in a project to encourage women to fill leadership roles, especially along the political pipeline.

Two decades ago, the late Elizabeth Janeway, an intellectual doyenne of the women's movement, fantasized the first woman president. She would be a vice president chosen to "balance" the ticket, a conservative Republican who ascends to the Oval Office denying any connection to feminism.

Today, television producers still must fantasize a "Commander in Chief." Mackenzie Allen [the leading character in a TV drama about a woman president] is also an accidental president, an independent who stood up for women by refusing to stand down from office. If,

Rosa Parks's leadership role in the Civil Rights Movement is debated by some. (**Joe Holloway Jr./Associated Press.**)

at times, the show is more about working motherhood than the presidency—Lynette of "Desperate Housewives" meets Mackenzie of White Househusbands—is this the only place to "see" a woman president?

Last weekend [October 2005], [Secretary of State] Condoleezza Rice was in her hometown of Birmingham, Ala., marking another civil rights event—the church bombing that killed four girls, including one of her friends. Rice may insist she is not running for office, but others saw that weekend as a screen test. As Rice herself said repeatedly: "I can think of so many cases where things that seemed impossible one day seemed inevitable a bit later."

> 'Rosa Parks was not an accidental heroine.'

Meanwhile, in New York, Hillary Clinton says she is running for nothing but reelection to the Senate against the hapless candidacy of Jeanine Pirro. An entire library of books attack Hillary and then accuse her of being a polarizing figure. Nevertheless, every poll shows her as the front-runner for the Democratic nomination for president.

Both Hillary and Condi have done something new. They've passed the "competence test," a bar set much higher for women. There are few, fans or foes, who deny that the senator and the secretary of state are qualified to run for the highest office. But what about the other test? How does the political imperative to be ambitious gel with the cultural imperative to be "unassuming"? Does it put a brake on women who would be leaders?

Sally Weaver, the CEO of the Atlanta Women's Foundation, says we have to get over the "deficit model" of leadership, a routine focus on what is missing in a woman. We need instead to encourage risk-taking.

Indeed, sometimes women are better at providing support for each other's disappointments than ambitions, better at offering comfort than at urging risk.

There is something in the culture that still tells women to wait until they are asked—to run, to lead. Something that praises us more for "quiet dignity" than for dangerous acts of courage.

So we come back to Rosa Parks. "Rosa Parks was not an accidental heroine," says Marie Wilson, head of the White House Project. In her time and place, Parks, too, was a polarizing figure. She was a leader whose beliefs were honed in a moral framework and whose courage was rooted in a political support system.

Rosa Parks was "unassuming"—except that she rejected all the assumptions about her place in the world. Rosa Parks was a "simple woman"—except for a mind made up and fed up. She was "quiet"—except, of course, for one thing. Her willingness to say "no" changed the world.

Rosa Parks Was Not the First to Refuse to Move

Gary Younge

By 1955, many of Montgomery's activists were ready to consider a boycott of the city's buses to challenge the principle of segregation. The year before, the US Supreme Court had reached its decision in *Brown v. Board of Education*, which made the attempt to create "separate but equal" facilities for blacks and whites unconstitutional. It only remained for activists to find a particular incident that might attract widespread attention and lead to a legal challenge. The following selection tells the story of Claudette Colvin, who was forcibly removed from a Montgomery bus nine months before Rosa Parks suffered the same fate. Colvin, then only fifteen years old, came from a poor area in Montgomery and, as the author points out, had darker skin than many, more prosperous African Americans. Activists considered mounting their challenges around Colvin's case but eventually decided against it, especially when it became known that the young girl was pregnant. Rosa Parks, forty-two years old and quite respectable, proved to be a more appealing focus for a protest, leaders decided. However,

SOURCE. Gary Younge, "She Would Not Be Moved," *The Guardian*, December 16, 2000. Copyright © 2000 by Guardian Publications Ltd. All rights reserved. Reproduced by permission of Guardian News Service, LTD.

Colvin was one of four women who served as plaintiffs in a lawsuit, *Browder v. Gayle*, which eventually reached the US Supreme Court. Gary Younge is a staff writer for *The Guardian* newspaper in Great Britain. He has also taught at Brooklyn College in New York City.

This much we know. On Thursday, December 1, 1955, Rosa Parks, a 42-year-old black seamstress, boarded a bus in Montgomery, Alabama, after a hard day's work, took a seat and headed for home. The bus went three stops before several white passengers got on. The driver, James Blake, turned around and ordered the black passengers to go to the back of the bus, so that the whites could take their places. "Move y'all, I want those two seats," he yelled.

The bus froze. Blake persisted. "Y'all better make it light on yourselves and let me have those seats," he said.

The three black passengers sitting alongside Parks rose reluctantly. Parks stayed put. Blake approached her. "Are you going to stand up?" he asked.

"No," said Parks.

"Well, I'm going to have you arrested," he replied.

"You may do that," said Parks, who is now 87 and lives in Detroit [Parks died in 2005].

It was an exchange later credited with changing the racial landscape of America. Parks's arrest sparked a chain reaction that started the bus boycott that launched the civil rights movement that transformed the apartheid of America's southern states from a local idiosyncrasy to an international scandal. It was her individual courage that triggered the collective display of defiance that turned a previously unknown 26-year-old preacher, Martin Luther King, into a household name.

It was a journey not only into history but also mythology. "She was a victim of both the forces of history and the forces of destiny," said King, in a quote now displayed in the civil rights museum in Atlanta. "She had been tracked down by the zeitgeist—the spirit of the times." And, from there, the short distance to sanctity: they called her "Saint Rosa," "an angel walking," "a heaven-sent messenger." "She gave me the feeling that I was the Moses that God had sent to Pharaoh," said Fred Gray, the lawyer who went on to represent her.

> Rosa Parks was neither a victim nor a saint, but a long-standing political activist and feminist.

But somewhere en route they mislaid the truth. Rosa Parks was neither a victim nor a saint, but a long-standing political activist and feminist. Moreover, she was not the first person to take a stand by keeping her seat and challenging the system. Nine months before Parks's arrest, a 15-year-old girl, Claudette Colvin, was thrown off a bus in the same town and in almost identical circumstances.

Like Parks, she, too, pleaded not guilty to breaking the law. And, like Parks, the local black establishment started to rally support nationwide for her cause. But, unlike Parks, Colvin never made it into the civil rights hall of fame. Just as her case was beginning to catch the nation's imagination, she became pregnant. To the exclusively male and predominantly middle-class, church-dominated, local black leadership in Montgomery, she was a fallen woman. She fell out of history altogether.

A Poor Montgomery Neighborhood

King Hill, Montgomery, is the sepia South. In this small, elevated patch of town, black people sit out on wooden porches and watch an impoverished world go by. Broken-down cars sit outside tumble-down houses. The pace of life is so slow and the mood so mellow that local residents look as if they have been wading through molasses in a half-hearted attempt to catch up with the past 50 years.

"Middle-class blacks looked down on King Hill," says Colvin today. "We had unpaved streets and outside toilets. We used to have a lot of juke joints up there, and maybe men would drink too much and get into a fight. It wasn't a bad area, but it had a reputation." It is here, at 658 Dixie Drive, that Colvin, 61, was raised by a great aunt, who was a maid, and great uncle, who was a "yard boy," whom she grew up calling her parents.

Today, she sits in a diner in the Bronx, her pudding-basin haircut framing a soft face with a distant smile. Her voice is soft and high, almost shrill. The urban bustle surrounding her could not seem further away from King Hill. She now works as a nurses' aide at an old people's home in downtown Manhattan. She turns, watches, wipes, feeds and washes the elderly patients and offers them a gentle, consoling word when they become disoriented.

> [Claudette] Colvin was also very dark-skinned, which put her at the bottom of the social pile within the black community.

"I make up stories to convince them to stay in bed." Her rhythm is simple and lifestyle frugal. She works the night shift and sleeps "when the sleep falls on her" during the day. She shops with her workmates and watches action movies on video. Until recently, none of her workmates knew anything of her pioneering role in the civil rights movement.

But go to King Hill and mention her name, and the first thing they will tell you is that she was the first. They remember her as a confident, studious, young girl with a streak that was rebellious without being boisterous. "She was a bookworm," says Gloria Hardin, who went to school with Colvin and who still lives in King Hill. "Always studying and using long words."

"She was an A student, quiet, well-mannered, neat, clean, intelligent, pretty, and deeply religious," writes Jo Ann Robinson in her authoritative book, *The Montgomery Bus Boycott and the Women Who Started It.*

Colvin was also very dark-skinned, which put her at the bottom of the social pile within the black community—in the pigmentocracy of the South at the time, and even today, while whites discriminated against blacks on grounds of skin colour, the black community discriminated against each other in terms of skin shade. The lighter you were, it was generally thought, the better; the closer your skin tone was to caramel, the closer you were perceived to be to whatever power structure prevailed, and the more likely you were to attract suspicion from those of a darker hue.

From "high-yellas" to "coal-coloureds," it is a tension steeped not only in language but in the arts, from Harlem Renaissance novelist Nella Larsen's book, *Passing*, to Spike Lee's film, *School Daze*. "The light-skinned girls always thought they were better looking," says Colvin. "So did the teachers, too. That meant most of the dark complexion ones didn't like themselves."

Colvin's High School Ambitions

Not so Colvin. They had threatened to throw her out of the Booker T. Washington school for wearing her hair in plaits. As well as the predictable teenage fantasy of "marrying a baseball player", she also had strong political convictions. When Ms. Nesbitt, her 10th grade teacher, asked the class to write down what they wanted to be, she unfolded a piece of paper with Colvin's handwriting on it that said: "President of the United States."

"I wanted to go north and liberate my people," explains Colvin. "They did think I was nutty and crazy."

One incident in particular preoccupied her at the time—the plight of her schoolmate, Jeremiah Reeves. Reeves was a teenage grocery delivery boy who was found having sex with a white woman. The woman alleged rape; Reeves insisted it was consensual. Either way, he had violated the South's deeply ingrained taboo on interracial sex—Alabama only voted to legalise inter-

Some argue that Claudette Colvin, the first black person arrested for sitting in the white section of a Montgomery bus, was unfairly treated by black leaders. (Julie Jacobson/Associated Press.)

racial marriage last month [November 2000] (the state held a referendum at the same time as the ballot for the US presidency), and then only by a 60–40 majority. "When I was in the ninth grade, all the police cars came to get Jeremiah," says Colvin. "They put him on death row." Four years later, they executed him.

It was this dark, clever, angry young woman who boarded the Highland Avenue bus on Friday, March 2, 1955, opposite Martin Luther King's church on Dexter Avenue, Montgomery. Colvin took her seat near the emergency door next to one black girl; two others sat across the aisle from her. The law at the time designated seats for black passengers at the back and for whites at the front, but left the middle as a murky no man's land. Black people were allowed to occupy those seats so long as white people didn't need them. If one white person wanted to sit down there, then all the black people on that row were supposed to get up and either stand or move further to the back.

> 'I didn't get up, because I didn't feel like I was breaking the law.'

As more white passengers got on, the driver asked black people to give up their seats. The three other girls got up; Colvin stayed put. "If it had been for an old lady, I would have got up, but it wasn't. I was sitting on the last seat that they said you could sit in. I didn't get up, because I didn't feel like I was breaking the law."

To complicate matters, a pregnant black woman, Mrs. Hamilton, got on and sat next to Colvin. The driver caught a glimpse of them through his mirror. "He asked us both to get up. [Mrs. Hamilton] said she was not going to get up and that she had paid her fare and that she didn't feel like standing," recalls Colvin. "So I told him I was not going to get up, either. So he said, 'If you are not going to get up, I will get a policeman.'"

The atmosphere on the bus became very tense. "We just sat there and waited for it all to happen," says Gloria Hardin, who was on the bus, too. "We didn't know what was going to happen, but we knew something would happen."

Colvin's Removal from the Bus

Almost 50 years on, Colvin still talks about the incident with a mixture of shock and indignation—as though she still cannot believe that this could have happened to her. She says she expected some abuse from the driver, but nothing more. "I thought he would stop and shout and then drive on. That's what they usually did."

But while the driver went to get a policeman, it was the white students who started to make noise. "You got to get up," they shouted. "She ain't got to do nothing but stay black and die," retorted a black passenger.

The policeman arrived, displaying two of the characteristics for which white Southern men had become renowned: gentility and racism. He could not bring himself to chide Mrs. Hamilton in her condition, but he could not allow her to stay where she was and flout the law as he understood it, either. So he turned on the black men sitting behind her. "If any of you are not gentlemen enough to give a lady a seat, you should be put in jail yourself," he said.

A sanitation worker, Mr. Harris, got up, gave her his seat and got off the bus. That left Colvin. "Aren't you going to get up?" asked the policeman.

"No," said Colvin.

He asked again.

"No, sir," she said.

"Oh God," wailed one black woman at the back. One white woman defended Colvin to the police; another said that, if she got away with this, "they will take over."

"I will take you off," said the policeman, then he kicked her. Two more kicks soon followed.

For all her bravado, Colvin was shocked by the extremity of what happened next. "It took on the form of harassment. I was very hurt, because I didn't know that white people would act like that and I . . . I was crying," she says. The policeman grabbed her and took her to a patrolman's car in which his colleagues were waiting. "What's going on with these n-----s?" asked one. Another cracked a joke about her bra size.

"I was really afraid, because you just didn't know what white people might do at that time," says Colvin. In August that year, a 14-year-old boy called Emmet Till had said, "Bye, baby," to a woman at a store in nearby Mississippi, and was fished out of the nearby Tallahatchie river a few days later, dead with a bullet in his skull, his eye gouged out and one side of his forehead crushed. "I didn't know if they were crazy, if they were going to take me to a Klan meeting. I started protecting my crotch. I was afraid they might rape me."

They took her to City Hall, where she was charged with misconduct, resisting arrest and violating the city segregation laws. The full enormity of what she had done was only just beginning to dawn on her. "I went bipolar. I knew what was happening, but I just kept trying to shut it out."

She concentrated her mind on things she had been learning at school. "I recited Edgar Allan Poe, Annabel Lee, the characters in *Midsummer Night's Dream*, the Lord's Prayer and the 23rd Psalm." Anything to detach herself from the horror of reality. Her pastor was called and came to pick her up. By the time she got home, her parents already knew. Everybody knew.

"The news travelled fast," wrote Robinson. "In a few hours, every Negro youngster on the streets discussed Colvin's arrest. Telephones rang. Clubs called special meetings and discussed the event with some degree of alarm. Mothers expressed concern about permitting their children on the buses. Men instructed their wives to walk or to share rides in neighbour's autos."

It was going to be a long night on Dixie Drive. "Nobody slept at home because we thought there would be some retaliation," says Colvin. An ad hoc committee headed by the most prominent local black activist, E.D. Nixon, was set up to discuss the possibility of making Colvin's arrest a test case. They sent a delegation to see the commissioner, and after a few meetings they appeared to have reached an understanding that the harassment would stop and that Colvin would be allowed to clear her name.

When the trial was held, Colvin pleaded innocent but was found guilty and released on indefinite probation in her parents' care. "She had remained calm all during the days of her waiting period and during the trial," wrote

Robinson. "But when she was found guilty, her agonised sobs penetrated the atmosphere of the courthouse."

Support and Rejection of Colvin

Nonetheless, the shock waves of her defiance had reverberated throughout Montgomery and beyond. Letters of support came from as far afield as Oregon and California. She still has one—a handwritten note from William Harris in Sacramento. It reads: "The wonderful thing which you have just done makes me feel like a craven coward. How encouraging it would be if more adults had your courage, self-respect and integrity. Respectfully and faithfully yours."

But even as she inspired awe throughout the country, elders within Montgomery's black community began to doubt her suitability as a standard-bearer of the movement. "I told Mrs. Parks, as I had told other leaders in Montgomery, that I thought the Claudette Colvin arrest was a good test case to end segregation on the buses," says Fred Gray, Parks's lawyer. "However, the black leadership in Montgomery at the time thought that we should wait."

Some in Montgomery, particularly in King Hill, think the decision was informed by snobbery. "It was partly because of her colour and because she was from the working poor," says Gwen Patton, who has been involved in civil rights work in Montgomery since the early 60s. "She lived in a little shack. It was a case of 'bourgey' [middle-class] blacks looking down on the working-class blacks."

"They never thought much of us, so there was no way they were going to run with us," says Hardin. Others say it is because she was a foul-mouthed tearaway. "It bothered some that there was an unruly, tomboy quality to Colvin, including a propensity for curse words and immature outbursts," writes Douglas Brinkley, who recently com-

> It was news of [Colvin's] pregnancy that ultimately persuaded the local black hierarchy to abandon her as a cause célèbre.

pleted a biography of Parks. But people in King Hill do not remember Colvin as that type of girl, and the accusation irritates Colvin to this day. "I never swore when I was young," she says. "Never."

Everyone, including Colvin, agreed that it was news of her pregnancy that ultimately persuaded the local black hierarchy to abandon her as a cause célèbre. For Colvin, the entire episode was traumatic: "Nowadays, you'd call it statutory rape, but back then it was just the kind of thing that happened," she says, describing the conditions under which she conceived. She refused to name the father or have anything to do with him. "When I told my mother I was pregnant, I thought she was going to have a heart attack. If I had told my father who did it, he would have killed him."

A personal tragedy for her was seen as a political liability by the town's civil rights leaders. In his Pulitzer prize-winning account of the civil rights years, *Parting the Waters*, Taylor Branch wrote: "Even if Montgomery Negroes were willing to rally behind an unwed, pregnant teenager—which they were not—her circumstances would make her an extremely vulnerable standard bearer."

"If the white press got a hold of that information, they would have [had] a field day," said Rosa Parks. "They'd call her a bad girl, and her case wouldn't have a chance." Montgomery's black establishment leaders decided they would have to wait for the right person. And that person, it transpired, would be Rosa Parks. "Mrs. Parks was a married woman," said E.D. Nixon. "She was morally clean, and she had a fairly good academic training. . . . If there was ever a person we would've been able to [use to] break the situation that existed on the Montgomery city line, Rosa L. Parks was the woman to use. . . . I probably would've examined a dozen more before I got there if Rosa Parks hadn't come along before I found the right one." . . .

Other Boycotts

Montgomery was not home to the first bus boycott any more than Colvin was the first person to challenge segregation. Two years earlier, in Baton Rouge, Louisiana, African-Americans launched an effective bus boycott after drivers refused to honour an integrated seating policy, which was settled in an unsatisfactory fudge. And, like the pregnant Mrs. Hamilton, many African-Americans refused to tolerate the indignity of the South's racist laws in silence.

Nor was Colvin the last to be passed over. In the nine months between her arrest and that of Parks, another young black woman, Mary Louise Smith, suffered a similar fate. Smith was arrested in October 1955, but was also not considered an appropriate candidate for a broader campaign—E.D. Nixon claimed that her father was a drunkard; Smith insists he was teetotaler [a non-drinker].

But there were two things about Colvin's stand on that March day that made it significant. First, it came less than a year after the US supreme court had outlawed the "separate but equal" policy that had provided the legal basis for racial segregation—what had been custom and practice in the South for generations was now against federal law and could be challenged in the courts.

Second, she was the first person, in Montgomery at least, to take up the challenge. "She was not the first person to be arrested for violation of the bus seating ordinance," said J. Mills Thornton, an author and academic. "But according to [the commissioner], she was the first person ever to enter a plea of not guilty to such a charge."

It is a rare, and poor, civil rights book that covers the Montgomery bus boycott and does not mention Claudette Colvin. But it is also a rare and excellent one that gives her more than a passing, dismissive mention. However, not one has bothered to interview her. Most Americans, even in Montgomery, have never heard of her. She has literally become a foot-note in history.

For we like our history neat—an easy-to-follow, self-contained narrative with dates, characters and landmarks with which we can weave together otherwise unrelated events into one apparently seamless length of fabric held together by sequence and consequence. Complexity, with all its nuances and shaded realities, is a messy business. So we choose the facts to fit the narrative we want to hear.

> By Monday, the day the boycott began, Colvin had already been airbrushed from the official version of events.

Civil Rights Leaders Spotlight Parks

While this does not happen by conspiracy, it is often facilitated by collusion. In this respect, the civil rights movement in Montgomery moved fast. Rosa Parks was thrown off the bus on a Thursday; by Friday, activists were distributing leaflets that highlighted her arrest as one of many, including those of Colvin and Mary Louise Smith: "Another Negro woman has been arrested and thrown in jail because she refused to get up out of her seat on the bus for a white person to sit down," they read. "It is the second time since the Claudette Colvin case that a Negro woman has been arrested for the same thing."

By Monday, the day the boycott began, Colvin had already been airbrushed from the official version of events. Meanwhile, Parks had been transformed from a politically-conscious activist to an upstanding, unfortunate Everywoman. "And since it had to happen, I'm happy it happened to a person like Mrs. Parks," said Martin Luther King from the pulpit of the Holt Street Baptist Church.

"For nobody can doubt the boundless outreach of her integrity. Nobody can doubt the height of her character, nobody can doubt the depth of her Christian commitment and devotion to the teachings of Jesus." Though he didn't say it, nobody was going to say that about the then heavily pregnant Colvin.

But Colvin was not the only casualty of this distortion. Parks was, too. Her casting as the prim, ageing, guileless seamstress with her hair in a bun who just happened to be in the wrong place at the right time denied her track record of militancy and feminism. She appreciated, but never embraced, King's strategy of nonviolent resistance, remains a keen supporter of Malcolm X and was constantly frustrated by sexism in the movement. "I had almost a life history of being rebellious against being mistreated against my colour," she said.

But the very spirit and independence of mind that had inspired Parks to challenge segregation started to pose a threat to Montgomery's black male hierarchy, which had started to believe, and then resent, their own spin. Nixon referred to her as a "lovely, stupid woman"; ministers would greet her at church functions with irony, "Well, if it isn't the superstar." Reverend Ralph Abernathy, who played a key role as King's right-hand man throughout the civil rights years, referred to her as a "tool" of the movement.

Those who are aware of these distortions in the civil rights story are few. Betty Shabbaz, the widow of Malcolm X, was one of them. In a letter published shortly before Shabbaz's death, she wrote to Parks with both praise and perspective: "'Standing up' was not even being the first to protest that indignity. Fifteen-year-old Claudette Colvin was the first to be arrested in protest of bus segregation in Montgomery.

"When Ed Nixon and the Women's Political Council of Montgomery recognised that you could be that hero, you met the challenge and changed our lives forever. It was not your tired feet, but your strength of character and resolve that inspired us." It is a letter Colvin knew nothing about.

Claudette Colvin Remembers

Colvin is not exactly bitter. But, as she recalls her teenage years after the arrest and the pregnancy, she hovers between resentment, sadness and bewilderment at the way she was treated. "They just dropped me. None of them spoke to me; they didn't see if I was okay. They never came and discussed it with my parents. They just didn't want to know me."

She believes that, if her pregnancy had been the only issue, they would have found a way to overcome it. "It would have been different if I hadn't been pregnant, but if I had lived in a different place or been light-skinned, it would have made a difference, too. They would have come and seen my parents and found me someone to marry."

When the boycott was over and the African-American community had emerged victorious, King, Nixon and Parks appeared for the cameras. "It's interesting that Claudette Colvin was not in the group, and rarely, if ever, rode a bus again in Montgomery," wrote Frank Sikora, an Alabama-based academic and author. After her arrest and late appearance in the court hearing, she was more or less forgotten. Later, she would tell a reporter that she would sometimes attend the rallies at the churches. "I would sit in the back and no one would even know I was there."

The upshot was that Colvin was left in an incredibly vulnerable position. A poor, single, pregnant, black, teenage mother who had both taken on the white establishment and fallen foul of the black one. It is this that incenses Patton. "I respect my elders, but I don't respect what they did to Colvin," she says. "For a while, there was a real distance between me and Mrs. Parks over this. Colvin was a kid. She needed support."

If that were not enough, the son, Raymond, to whom she would give birth in December, emerged light-skinned: "He came out looking kind of yellow, and then I was ostracised because I wouldn't say who the father was and they thought it was a white man. He wasn't." She became quiet and withdrawn. "I wasn't with it at all. All I could do is cry."

Robinson recalls: "She needed encouragement, for since her conviction as a law violator her head was not held so high. She did not look people straight in the eye as before." She received a scholarship to the local, historically black university, Alabama State, even though the college authorities were none too keen on having a "troublemaker" on campus.

Inescapable Humility

The tears kept coming. She dropped out. She could not find work in Montgomery because as soon as white people found out what she had done, they fired her. "I just couldn't get a job. I'd change my name so that I could work in a restaurant, and they'd find out who I was and that was it. I ran out of identities." Even when she did get work, it was humiliating. "I had this baby of my own and yet I had to leave him with my mother so I could babysit for white people who hated me."

In the space of a few years, a confident A-grade student had passed through the eye of a political storm and emerged a bedraggled outcast. "It changed my life," she says. "I became aware of how the world is and how the white establishment plays black people against each other."

> 'They wanted someone who would shake hands and go to banquets . . . someone they could control, and they knew . . . they couldn't control me.'

She believes, however, that they were right to choose someone such as Rosa Parks as a standard-bearer. "They picked the right person. They needed someone who could bring together all the classes. They wouldn't have followed me. They wanted someone who would shake hands and go to banquets. They wanted someone they could control, and they knew, as a teenager, they couldn't control me."

But she also believes that they were wrong not to support her in her time of need. "They weren't there for me when I tried to make a comeback. I thought maybe they would help me get a degree, or talk to someone about getting me work. I thought they could get me together with Rosa Parks and we could go out together and talk to children."

Similarly, Patton believes that the pragmatic decision not to put Colvin in the spotlight at first was probably correct, but that it does not excuse a wilful negligence to acknowledge her contribution afterwards. "I have no problem with them not lifting up Colvin in 1955. I have a problem with them not lifting her up in 1970. Rosa Parks could have said many times [in the intervening years] 'And there were others.'"

Life After Montgomery

Colvin's life after Montgomery is a metaphor for postwar black America. As the struggle moved from civil rights to economic rights, Colvin followed the route of the great migration and went north to a low-paid job and urban deprivation. She left Montgomery for New York in 1958 to work as a live-in domestic and soon became accustomed to the differences and similarities between north and south.

While the power relationship of maid and madam was the same, she encountered less petty racism and institutionalised indignity in the north. In the south, a live-in domestic would never dream of washing her own clothes with those of her employers. So when she came down one day to find her employer's laundry dumped on top of hers with a polite request to wash them at the same time, she was shocked. "That's when I knew I was out of the South. That could just never have happened there."

At the start, she occasionally travelled back to Montgomery by bus with baby Raymond to see her parents and look for work in a place where her family could lend support, but no one would employ her. A year later, she fell pregnant again, and in 1960 gave birth to Randy. The pressure of making ends meet in the urban north with two infants and no family became too much.

In what was a common arrangement at the time, she left Raymond and Randy with her mother in Montgomery as she sought work in the north. Things got tough. A couple of times she even considered going into prostitution. "The only thing that kept me out of it was the other things that go with it. Stealing, drugging people. I figured that after the first time the physical thing wouldn't matter so much, but I couldn't get involved in all the other stuff."

At one and the same time, she had become both more independent and more vulnerable, and looking for some evidence for the gains of the civil rights era in her own life. "What we got from that time was what was on the books anyhow. Working-class people were the foot soldiers, but where are they now—they haven't seen any progress. It was the middle classes who were able to take advantage of the laws."

Her two boys took wildly divergent paths. Like many African-American men, Raymond, the unborn child she was carrying during the heady days of 1955, joined the US army. Like all too many, he later became involved in drugs and died of an overdose in her apartment. Like many others, Randy emerged successful and moved back down south, to Atlanta, where he now works as an accountant. Colvin has five grandchildren.

> 'There is no closure. This does not belong in a museum, because this struggle is not over.'

Earlier this month [December 2000], Troy State University opened a Rosa Parks museum in Montgomery to honour the small town's place in civil rights history on its 45th anniversary. Roy White, who was responsible for much of what went into the museum, called Colvin to ask if she would appear in a video to tell her story. She refused. "They've already called it the Rosa Parks museum, so they've already made up their minds what the story is."

He suggested that maybe she would achieve some closure by participating. "What closure can there be for me?" she asks with exasperation. "There is no closure. This does not belong in a museum, because this struggle is not over. We still don't have all that we should have. And, personally, there can be no closure. They took away my life. If they want closure, they should give it to my grandchildren."

Martin Luther King Jr. Was Always Committed to Nonviolence

Deanna Proach

The Montgomery Bus Boycott was an important moment in the civil rights movement for many reasons. One was that it was characterized by nonviolent protest, a feature that helped to form the larger civil rights effort for many years. Indeed, the boycott's leaders, notably Martin Luther King Jr., insisted that the boycotters refrain not only from violence but also from insults and other means that might reduce the dignity and morality of their cause. In the following selection, the author suggests that King developed his commitment to nonviolence while a seminary student in Pennsylvania from 1948 to 1951. There he studied the teachings and actions of Mohandas Gandhi, whose leadership of nonviolent mass protests had helped India to gain its independence from Great Britain in the 1930s and 1940s. King was ready, when the need arose, to bring similar tactics to Montgomery and the civil rights movement. Deanna Proach is a Canadian author.

SOURCE. Deanna Proach, "Martin Luther King: The Philosophy of Nonviolent Resistance," Suite101.com, January 1, 2009. All rights reserved. Reproduced by permission.

From 1956 until his assassination in 1968, Martin Luther King Junior, the son of a Baptist preacher, was the dominant leader in African Americans' quest for civil rights and a better life in general. Martin Luther King firmly believed the power of love, essential to his idea of nonviolent resistance, could serve as the most effective weapon against a racist and unjust social system. His method of nonviolent resistance greatly helped his people achieve freedom and fairer treatment in later years to come.

King Studies the Philosophy of Nonviolent Resistance

Prior to becoming a civil rights leader, King attended Cozer Theological Seminary in Pennsylvania. Throughout his studies Martin studied a number of famous theologians, but none appealed more to him than [Indian independence leader Mohandas] Gandhi's teachings on nonviolence. Coming from a Christian Baptist family, King believed the love ethic of Jesus Christ can be applied to the conflict between the African Americans and the white communities in the United States. King firmly maintained that guidance from a loving God equipped with the idea of nonviolence is the only solution to ending racial discrimination against his people and in helping his people achieve civil rights.

Shortly after receiving his doctorate degree, he received a pastorate position at the Dexter Avenue Baptist Church in Montgomery, Alabama. After settling in, King immediately put his idea of nonviolent resistance into action.

King's Key Points About the Philosophy of Nonviolence

As pastor and civil rights leader, King affirmed six key points about the philosophy of nonviolence. First, he argued that, even though nonviolence is commonly portrayed as cowardly, it is not. The nonviolent protestor, according to King, uses his mind to effectively convince the opponent that he is in the wrong. It also requires great emotional and spiritual courage to stand up against injustice.

Second, the nonviolent protestor does not seek to disgrace the opponent, but to seek his understanding and friendship. This principle worked in King's organized boycott of the Montgomery bus system after an African American woman, Rosa Parks, refused to give her seat to a white man. The boycott led the Supreme Court to render the Alabama laws of segregation on public transit as unconstitutional.

Thirdly, nonviolence is directed against evil, not the people who are committing the evil. The fight was not between two races, but between justice and injustice.

Fourth, nonviolent resistance is a willingness to accept suffering without retaliating. Retaliatory violence would only cause more chaos, trauma and hatred. After his house was bombed by violent white protestors during the Montgomery bus boycott, King reminded his angry people that they must love their white brothers regardless of their actions. Accepting suffering would lead to a change in heart and mind of the opponent.

> Nonviolent resistance is powerful in that it can overcome all bitterness and hatred and replace them with love.

Martin's fifth key point on nonviolence was that God is always on the side of truth. Therefore, the African American activists should keep faith that justice will happen in the future.

The sixth key point was most central to Martin's method of nonviolent resistance. He believed that nonviolent resistance prevented physical and emotional violence. The method of nonviolent resistance is powerful in that it can overcome all bitterness and hatred and replace them with love.

Passive Resistance and Nonviolent Protest

The Montgomery Bus Boycott was the first instance of large-scale nonviolent protest in US history. Many leaders and historians credited not only its success but its long-term influence to the fact that protesters not only acted nonviolently but held their heads up with quiet dignity while doing so.

The success of these tactics was a validation of the teachings and leadership of Martin Luther King Jr., who at the time of the boycott was a Montgomery pastor just emerging as a civil rights leader. While studying for the ministry, King had learned of the teachings of such advocates of nonviolence as Henry David Thoreau, a nineteenth-century essayist, and Mohandas Gandhi, a leader of India's independence movement. It is likely that Gandhi's tactics were most instructive for King and the Montgomery protesters.

Gandhi had demonstrated that, through the use of nonviolent resistance, protesters could establish a sort of moral authority over their opponents as well as gain sympathy from observers. The point of protests was not simply to win, argued Gandhi, but to bring your opponents over to your cause: to change their hearts. Violence, in Gandhi's view, only inspired further violence. When faced with threats, protesters should refuse the temptation to strike back. In addition, Gandhi argued, protesters should be ready to face jail terms or even beatings, but with the understanding that they would ultimately win. In the 1920s, '30s, and '40s, Gandhi himself led many nonviolent protests and served months in jail, but his efforts helped turn Indian independence into a global cause that finally resulted, in 1947, in the end of its status as a British colony and its emergence as the world's largest democracy.

The Montgomery Bus Boycott was a large-scale implementation of the Gandhian tactic of passive resistance; knowing that their cause was right, protesters simply refused to participate in the behavior that oppressed them. Thanks largely to King's insistence, boycotters did not strike out at those who attacked them, nor did they complain much about the difficulties of not riding the bus. They knew that, eventually, and through legal means, segregation on Montgomery's buses would come to an end. Martin Luther King Jr., for his part, continued to emphasize nonviolence as a civil rights leader after the boycott ended. And like Gandhi, he served jail terms and faced many attacks, but refused to answer violence with violence.

Mohandas Gandhi's commitment to non-violent mass protests was an early inspiration for Martin Luther King Jr. (**Elliott & Fry/Stringer/ Getty Images.**)

The Power of King's Method of Nonviolent Resistance

King's method of nonviolent resistance did eventually help his people gain justice and equal civil rights. His tragic assassination in April of 1968 not only led to a series of riots across the nation, it caused many people to realize the power and purity of King's method of nonviolent resistance. King's nonviolent advocacy of a program of moderation and inclusion in the face of violence led future generations to revere him as a humble and honourable civil rights leader and a national hero. Shortly after his assassination, President [Lyndon B.] Johnson declared a national mourning day in his honour. Nine years later, in 1977, President [Jimmy] Carter awarded Martin Luther King the Presidential Medal of Freedom.

King Dedicated Himself to Nonviolent Protest Because of Violent Events in Montgomery

Stephan Thernstrom and Abigail Thernstrom

In the following selection, two historians argue that Martin Luther King Jr. only committed himself to nonviolent tactics in the Montgomery Bus Boycott following an attack on his home in January 1956, nearly two months after the beginning of the protest. Indeed, they note, King had once suspected that the fight for equality might require an armed revolt, and he kept a gun at his home. But as the boycott extended past its first weeks, its importance and implications increased. White Montgomerians tried to end the boycott by various means, including the arrest of leaders, and the event gained national attention. As tensions rose and threats and attacks increased, King grew fearful that any turn

SOURCE. Stephan Thernstrom and Abigail Thernstrom, *America in Black and White: One Nation, Indivisible.* New York: Simon & Schuster, 1997, pp. 109–112. Copyright © 1997 by Stephan Thernstrom and Abigail Thernstrom. All rights reserved. Reproduced by permission of Writer's Representatives. In North America by permission of Simon & Schuster Macmillan.

to violence might lead to failure and revenge. He then emphasized the need for protesters to maintain the moral high ground by using the nonviolent tactics he had studied while a student at Crozer Theological Seminary in Pennsylvania and at the Boston University School of Divinity. Stephan Thernstrom is the Winthrop Research Professor of History at Harvard University. Abigail Thernstrom is vice-chair of the United States Commission for Civil Rights. Together and separately they have written many books and articles on civil rights.

Among the black clergymen who joined in the debate on how to respond to the jailing of Rosa Parks was a twenty-six-year-old graduate of the Boston University Divinity School who had recently taken up the pulpit at the Dexter Avenue Baptist Church—the Reverend Martin Luther King, Jr. When an organization to carry out the bus boycott was formed—the Montgomery Improvement Association—King was named its head. He was a newcomer to Montgomery, but that seeming liability was in fact an asset. He had not been in town long enough to have made many friends—or many enemies.

Under King's leadership, what started as a one-day gesture of protest against the mistreatment of black people on local buses became a major long-term commitment, supported by almost the entire black community, which accounted for 37 percent of the city's population and about three-fourths of its regular bus patrons. When the initial boycott produced no response from local authorities, the Montgomery Improvement Association pledged (from its position of extraordinary strength) that it would continue until black passengers were assured of better treatment. The sight of empty buses rolling through black neighborhoods led one woman to remark gleefully that the buses that went by her door were "as naked as can be." Car pools were organized to take care of those in desperate need of a ride, but most of

> [King] told his fellow blacks that change would never come unless they had the courage to stand up for their rights, regardless of the cost.

the boycotters simply walked to their destinations. The Montgomery police did their best to put the car pools out of business by arresting drivers for petty, sometimes altogether imaginary, traffic violations. King himself was hauled off to jail on one occasion for allegedly driving at thirty miles an hour in a twenty-five-mile-an-hour zone. But these efforts at harassment were ineffective.

Meeting the Challenge

At a mass meeting called to decide whether to continue the boycott, King warned whites that a new day was dawning—that blacks would no longer tolerate being treated as second-class citizens. And he told his fellow blacks that change would never come unless they had the courage to stand up for their rights, regardless of the cost. "We are here this evening," he declared,

> to say to those who have mistreated us so long that we are tired—tired of being segregated and humiliated; tired of being kicked about by the brutal feet of oppression. We had no alternative but to protest. For many years we have shown amazing patience. . . . But we come here tonight to be saved from that patience that makes us patient with anything less than freedom and justice.

Although this was a radical and unflinching challenge to the principle of white supremacy, the concrete changes the organizers of the boycott sought at the outset were remarkably modest. King spoke passionately of the need to obtain justice on the buses of this city," but by "justice" he did not mean an entirely desegregated bus system. The principal demand of the boycotters at this point was only that Montgomery adopt the somewhat milder form of segregation that was used on the buses in

Mobile, Alabama. In Mobile your race determined where you were allowed to sit when you first boarded, but no African American was required to move after having settled into a seat.

The boycott began, then, as a call for better treatment within the framework of "separate but equal." Its organizers launched no principled attack against the whole notion of assigning seats on a bus on the basis of race. In fact, it could even be argued that their demands, by making the system seem a bit more fair, would have given the segregation some additional life. That is precisely why the NAACP [National Association for the Advancement of Colored People] refused at first to help with Mrs. [Rosa] Parks's appeal. The organization would not intervene in a case that seemed to be "asking merely for more polite segregation." . . .

Montgomery Officials Fight Back

The protest escalated into a fight for the complete abolition of bus segregation only after two months of futile negotiations with city authorities made their intransigence all too clear. The bus company itself might have welcomed a settlement; with 75 percent of its patrons walking to work, it was running in the red. Privately owned, it was dedicated not to the cause of segregation but to its financial bottom line. . . . But the politicians didn't care about the company's balance sheet. They cared about votes—that is, white votes. And whites, with few exceptions, had no sympathy for black demands. In fact, the mayor, all three members of the city commission, and several other public officials belonged to the local chapter of the Citizens' Council, whose membership quickly reached 12,000, more than a quarter of Montgomery's adult white population. Not surprisingly, these officials were determined not to give an inch.

The possibility of reaching a negotiated settlement vanished altogether after a grand jury issued criminal indictments against no fewer than eighty-nine of Montgomery's black citizens (twenty-four of them ministers) for conspiring to boycott in violation of a 1921 statute. But again, the attempt at repression only strengthened the protest effort. For the first time, the Montgomery story became front-page news in several national newspapers, which in turn increased the flow of outside contributions to the movement.

Once it was agreed that the objective was to abolish segregation, not to make it a little more comfortable, the NAACP's lawyers were happy to do the necessary legal work. Shifting the struggle into a federal courtroom was a momentous and revealing development. Southerners had always insisted that they were capable of resolving racial conflict without the interference of outsiders—judges, in this instance. But the surge of white rage that led to the mushrooming of Citizens' Councils poisoned the political climate; the South, in fact, did not have the capacity to save itself.

> King became a convinced advocate of nonviolence only after experiencing violence directed against his wife and infant daughter.

A Violent Inspiration for Nonviolent Resistance

It was during the Montgomery boycott that Martin Luther King first articulated the principle of nonviolent resistance so integral to the success of the civil rights movement. And yet it is important to recall that King was not fully committed to nonviolence when the Montgomery struggle began. Although he had been attracted to Gandhian ideas [Indian leader Mohandas Gandhi's advocacy of nonviolence] in his student days, in 1955 he apparently believed that "the only way we could solve our problem of segregation was an armed revolt." Painfully aware that black men who defied southern racial mores

could expect to be the victims of violence, he had armed guards to protect his residence, and kept a gun at home.

King became a convinced advocate of nonviolence only after experiencing violence directed against his wife and infant daughter. On January 30, 1956, just a few hours after the Montgomery Improvement Association decided to sue the city in federal court, a stick of dynamite exploded on his front porch. No one was hurt, but a furious crowd of blacks, many of them armed, quickly gathered outside the house. King, who had been off at a

Rev. Ralph David Abernathy left a Montgomery jail on February 22, 1956. He was one of 89 citizens indicted for conspiracy to boycott. (**Associated Press.**)

meeting, arrived on the scene to hear one of his supporters tell a policeman, "You got your .38 and I got mine, so let's battle it out." The incident drove home the obvious point that "an armed revolt" would mean blacks pitted against a white population that outnumbered them ten to one. Rejecting violence as an instrument not only gave civil rights advocates the moral high ground; it was a pragmatic necessity. King calmed the angry crowd that night by warning that "he who lives by the sword will perish by the sword"; "love your enemies," "meet hate with love," he urged. He disarmed his own guards and got rid of his gun.

The boycott finally came to an end after 381 days, but not because either side had lost its will to fight. In June 1956 a three-judge federal panel ruled that the racial segregation of Montgomery's buses was unconstitutional, and in November the Supreme Court affirmed the decision. The boycott officially continued until December 21, 1956, when the court order took effect and King and other supporters of the movement, black and white, boarded a bus and occupied the front seats.

The rage that the boycott had stirred up did not suddenly evaporate with the legal decision. Two days after integrated buses started running, in the middle of the night, someone fired a shotgun through King's front door. A few days later snipers fired upon three buses. More than a dozen prominent blacks had their cars splashed with acid. In early January 1957 four black churches and the homes of both Ralph Abernathy [a local minister and activist] and Robert Graetz (the leading local white minister in the Montgomery Improvement Association) were bombed. Two men were eventually arrested and tried for the bombings. But despite overwhelming physical evidence and their own confessions, a jury refused to convict them.

Montgomery's blacks had won a great victory, of course. But the victory could not be credited to the boycott. The courts would have rendered precisely the same verdict even if there had been no mass protest movement. From one perspective, a boycott in Baton Rouge, Louisiana, three years earlier had been much more successful. The city held out only ten days, and then decided to adopt a Mobile-style, first-come first-served segregation plan. But the Montgomery protest was of far greater historical significance. Not only did it achieve real desegregation; it started a movement that, in King's words, "would gain national recognition; whose echoes would ring in the ears of people of every nation; a movement that would astound the oppressor, and bring new hope to the oppressed."

The Supreme Court Affirms That Segregation on Montgomery's Buses Is Unconstitutional

Luther A. Huston

While black Montgomerians and their white supporters continued their boycott of the city's buses into 1956, civil rights lawyers sought to overturn segregation laws in the courts. Their main case was *Browder v. Gayle*, which pitted four women who had been forced to give up their seats—Aurelia Browder, Claudette Colvin, Susie McDonald, and Mary Louise Smith—against the city of Montgomery, as represented by Mayor W.A. Gayle. The case, first heard in a federal court in Alabama, resulted in a decision claiming that the Fourteenth Amendment rights of the four women had been violated. As the following selection notes, this decision was upheld by the US Supreme Court in November, 1956. The Fourteenth Amendment guarantees that all citizens have due process under the law as well as equal protection under the law. As the selection indicates, these guarantees had been adjusted in parts of the South to provide "separate but equal" facilities for blacks and whites, a feature made possible by the Supreme Court's *Plessy v. Ferguson* decision in 1896. But as the author of the selection, journalist Luther A. Huston, writes, the Supreme Court's decision in *Browder v. Gayle* would bring an end to "separate but equal." In Montgomery, blacks were able to ride fully integrated buses by the end of 1956.

An Alabama law and a city ordinance requiring segregation of races on intrastate buses were declared invalid by the Supreme Court today [November 13, 1956].

The Court affirmed a ruling by a three-judge Federal court that held the challenged statutes "violate the due process and equal protection clauses of the Fourteenth Amendment to the Constitution of the United States."

The Fourteenth Amendment provides that no state shall deprive any person of life, liberty, or property without due process of law nor deny to any citizen the equal protection of the laws.

> The ruling was interpreted as outlawing state or municipal enactments anywhere that require separation of the races on public vehicles.

In upholding the lower court's judgment, the Supreme Court cited its 1954 decision outlawing racial discrimination in public parks and on public golf courses.

Officials of several Southern states indicated they would continue to enforce bus segregation laws despite the court's decision. Segregationist leaders were bitter in their denunciations of the court and its ruling.

"Separate but Equal"

Although only Alabama laws were involved today, the ruling was interpreted as outlawing state or municipal enactments anywhere that require separation of the races on public vehicles. It was thought to have placed a headstone at the grave of Plessy v. Ferguson.

This was a case decided in 1896, in which the high court ruled that racial segregation on railroads was not unconstitutional if separate but equal facilities were provided.

The "separate but equal" doctrine later was applied to segregation in other fields, such as education, and generally prevailed until the high court's ruling in school cases.

Since then the doctrine has been discarded in every test that has been brought to the Supreme Court.

Arkansas, Florida, Georgia, Louisiana, Mississippi, Oklahoma, Tennessee and Texas have laws that could be affected by today's ruling.

Last term the Supreme Court had under advisement a case from Columbia, S.C. involving a similar issue. The Fourth Circuit Court of Appeals had invalidated South Carolina's bus segregation law. The ruling was interpreted as applying also to bus segregation in Virginia, West Virginia, North Carolina and Maryland, which are in the Fourth Judicial Circuit.

In that case, however, the Supreme Court dismissed the appeal on technical grounds, although it did not specifically affirm or reverse the circuit court's ruling.

Today's order left little doubt that a new appeal in the Columbia case, if it again came to the high court after procedural requirements had been compiled with in the lower courts, would suffer the fate of the Alabama statutes.

Legal Case Grew Out of Boycott

The ruling affirmed today grew out of a boycott by Negroes in Montgomery, Ala., of the local buses. The boycott began last year and is continuing.

Aurelia S. Browder, Susie McDonald, Claudette Colvin and Mary Louise Smith, Negroes, had been

required by bus drivers or the police to comply with segregation laws and had been arrested and fined for refusal to do so.

The Montgomery City code required bus operators to provide separate but equal accommodations for white and colored passengers. A state law also required segregation.

The four women did not appeal their convictions, but brought suit to challenge the constitutionality of the city code and the state law.

After the boycott, African Americans were allowed to use the front door of the bus. (Don Cravens/Contributor/Time & Life Pictures/Getty Images.)

A court composed of Circuit Judge Richard T. Rives and District Judges Frank M. Johnson Jr. and Seybourn H. Lynne heard the case. Judges Rives and Johnson held the challenged statues unconstitutional. Judge Lynne dissented.

The Alabama Public Service Commission and the Montgomery Board of Commissioners appealed to the Supreme Court. They asserted that the high court never had overruled the Plessy v. Ferguson decision. They urged the court to hear the case and give a clear-cut, written opinion disposing of the issue.

The court, however, merely granted a motion of lawyers for the Negroes that the lower court decision be affirmed.

John Patterson, Attorney General of Alabama, and Walter J. Knabe of Montgomery presented the appeals of the state and municipal bodies. The Negroes were represented by Thurgood Marshall, Robert L. Carter, Fred D. Gray and Charles D. Langford.

Slight Delay Is Foreseen

United Circuit Judge Richard T. Rives of Montgomery, Ala., said today the Supreme Court injunction against segregation on Montgomery buses would go into effect as soon as the court's order reached the United States District Court at Montgomery.

Customarily, an order takes two or three weeks to reach the district court, he said.

Judge Rives is in Fort Worth [Texas] for a session of the Fifth Circuit Court of Appeals. He is one of three special judges whose decision on bus segregation was upheld by the Supreme Court today.

A Judge Argues That Segregation on Montgomery's Buses Should Not Be Outlawed

Seybourn H. Lynne

The author of the following selection was one of the three judges in the panel that decided the case known as *Browder v. Gayle*. That case was brought by civil rights lawyers to end segregation on Montgomery's buses. While the other two judges on the Alabama district court panel, Richard T. Rives and Frank M. Johnson Jr., argued that such segregation was unconstitutional and should end, Judge Lynne offered a dissenting opinion. He argued that there was not enough reason to overturn the US Supreme Court's precedent set in 1896's *Plessy v. Ferguson* decision. This decision allowed states and municipalities to offer "separate but equal" facilities for blacks and whites and, to Lynne's mind, there had not been enough of a new trend in legal decisions to change

SOURCE. Seybourn H. Lynne, "Browder v. Gayle, 142 F. Supp. 707—Dist. Court, MD Alabama 1956," scholar.google.com, 1956.

a standing precedent. Second, Lynne argued that the Fourteenth Amendment to the US Constitution, upon which the majority opinion was based, had little to say about what freedoms individual states had to regulate commerce in such areas as Montgomery's privately owned bus system. Seybourn Harris Lynne was a judge in Alabama from 1934 until his death in 2000.

Only a profound, philosophical disagreement with the ultimate conclusion of the majority "that the separate but equal doctrine can no longer be safely followed as a correct statement of the law" would prompt this, my first dissent. But I should consider myself recreant both to conscience and duty in withholding my views because of the affection and esteem which I bear for my associates.

For many years as a trial judge in the state and federal systems I have endeavored faithfully to understand and apply precedents established by the opinions of appellate courts. This was not a blind obedience to a legalistic formula embodied in the rule of *stare decisis* [legal precedents]. It was the result of a simple belief that the laws which regulate the conduct, the affairs, and sometimes the emotions of our people should evidence not only the appearance but also the spirit of stability.

> A comparatively new principle of pernicious implications has found its way into our jurisprudence.

Judges of trial courts frequently find themselves in disagreement with the rationale of an old, but clearly controlling precedent. That is so because their positions do not insulate them from those changing physical and metaphysical concepts which form a part of the life process. But they are neither designed nor equipped to perform the legislative function of putting off the old and putting on the new. To arrogate to themselves this prerogative, in my humble opinion, would be the first, fatal step in making hollow the proud boast that ours is a "government of laws and not of men."

Judge [Richard T.] Rives, just the other day, delivering the opinion of the Court of Appeals for the Fifth Circuit, stated my position, clearly and concisely:

> In the face of such recognition by the Supreme Court of a test of criminal responsibility, we do not feel at liberty to consider and decide whether in our opinion the recent modification of such test in the District of Columbia is sound or unsound, nor whether some other test should be adopted. *This Circuit follows the law as stated by the Supreme Court and leaves any need for modification thereof to that Court.* (Emphasis supplied.) . . .

A comparatively new principle of pernicious implications has found its way into our jurisprudence. Lower courts may feel free to disregard the precise precedent of a Supreme Court opinion if they perceive a "pronounced new doctrinal trend" in its later decisions which would influence a cautious judge to prophesy that in due time and in a proper case such established precedent will be overturned explicitly. Peculiarly appropriate in this context is the following language of Judge Woodbury, writing for the First Circuit in *New England Mutual Life Ins. Co. v. Welch* [(1946)]:

> Furthermore we find no indication from anything said therein of a purpose to depart from the rule of the earlier decisions cited above. Under these circumstances we see no occasion even to consider the basic question whether we would adopt the doctrine of *Barnette v. West Virginia State Board of Education* [(1943)], and *Spector Motor Service v. Walsh* [(1943)], and in extraordinary situations disregard controlling decisions of the Supreme Court not yet explicitly overruled. It will suffice to say that we would feel disposed to consider taking such a course

only when there are the clearest indications that the controlling decision of the Supreme Court, though not formally overruled, would no longer be followed by that Court and we find no such indications here." . . .

No New Legal Precedent

Of course I appreciate the care with which the Supreme Court limits its pronouncements upon great constitutional questions to the narrow issues before it and the only issue in *Brown* [*v. Board of Education of Topeka* (1954)] involved a collision between the Fourteenth Amendment and state laws commanding segregation in the public schools. But in *Brown* the Court's opinion referred to *Plessy v. Ferguson* six times and to its "separate but equal" doctrine on four occasions. It epitomized its concept of that doctrine as follows: "Under that doctrine, equality of treatment is accorded when the races are provided substantially equal facilities, even though these facilities be separate." Its ultimate conclusion was, and this I conceive to be the rationale of its decision, "that in the field of public education the doctrine of 'separate but equal' has no place. Separate educational facilities are inherently unequal."

It seems to me that the Supreme Court therein recognized that there still remains an area within our constitutional scheme of state and federal governments wherein that doctrine may be applied even though its applications are always constitutionally suspect and for sixty years it may have been more honored in the breach than in the observance. Granted that the trend of its opinions is to the effect that segregation is not to be permitted in public facilities furnished by the state itself and the moneys of the state, as in the case of public schools, or public parks or municipal golf courses, on the plain theory that if the state is going to provide such facilities at all, it must provide them equally to the citizens, it does not follow that it

Photo on following page: Army soldiers were sent to Little Rock to ensure that the nine black students could enter the newly integrated school. (George Silk/Contributor/Time & Life Pictures/Getty Images.)

Integrating High Schools in Little Rock, Arkansas, 1957

The Montgomery Bus Boycott helped bring the attention of the nation and world to the civil rights movement then gathering momentum in the American South. It was quickly followed by another event of great drama and the threat of violence: the forced integration of public schools in Little Rock, Arkansas.

In *Brown v. Board of Education*, the US Supreme Court determined that localities could no longer legally segregate public schools. Although the court reached its decision in 1954, many places in the South were slow to implement integration. In Little Rock, the National Association for the Advancement of Colored People (NAACP) worked with local officials and school board members to place African American students in Little Rock Central High School beginning in September 1957. Nine black teenagers, the so-called Little Rock Nine, made their plans to be the first African Americans to attend the previously segregated school.

Arkansas governor Orval Faubus opposed not only the idea of school segregation but the notion that such measures be imposed on states by the federal government. He publicly threw his support behind segregationist groups who planned to block the students from even entering Little Rock Central High. Faubus even sent to the school armed members of the Arkansas National Guard to prevent the students from entering the building. Photographs, film footage, and news reports of armed men preventing teenagers from going to school quickly drew attention and sympathy from around the country and the world.

President Dwight D. Eisenhower, following a formal request from Little Rock's mayor, responded by not only asserting federal control over the Arkansas National Guard but also sending to the city soldiers from the US Army's 101st Airborne Division. Hundreds of troops, in other words, were brought in to ensure that the Little Rock Nine could attend high school. Although the students were fully enrolled by the end of September and finished the academic year, they continued to face threats from demonstrators outside the school building and occasional abuse from fellow students inside it.

may not be permitted in public utilities holding nonexclusive franchises.

If that doctrine has any vitality, this is such a case in which it has been applied fairly. According to its teaching, not absolute, but substantial equality is required. Such equality is not a question of dogma, but one of fact. Under the undisputed evidence adduced upon the hearing before us practices under the laws here attacked have resulted in providing the races not only substantially equal but in truth identical facilities. . . .

> The laws here attacked have resulted in providing the races not only substantially equal but in truth identical facilities.

The supremacy of the federal government in matters affecting interstate commerce is axiomatic. Cases involving the exercise of its power in that realm shed no light on Fourteenth Amendment problems. It does seem quite clear that by its terms the Congress is given the power and duty to enforce the Fourteenth Amendment by legislation. Thus the Congress would have the power, thus derived, to proscribe segregation in intrastate transportation. It is worthy of note that for sixty years it has not seen fit to do so.

While any student of history knows that under our system of government vindication of the constitutional rights of the individual is not, and ought not to be, entrusted to the Congress, its reticence to intrude upon the internal affairs of the several states should caution us against doing so where the path of duty is not plainly marked and when we must hold a clear precedent of the Supreme Court outmoded.

Because I would dismiss the action on the authority of *Plessy v. Ferguson*, I do not reach the procedural questions discussed in the majority opinion. I respectfully dissent.

The Bus Boycott Changed Montgomery Forever

Wilma Dykeman and James Stokely

The Montgomery Bus Boycott came to an end on December 21, 1956, a day described in the following selection. It ended with a victory for protesters in a Supreme Court decision arguing that segregation on the city's buses was a violation of the constitutional rights of African Americans. According to the authors of the selection, while many black Montgomerians were hesitant to boast about any great victory, the event nevertheless showed the power and influence that they had; the relations between the African American and white communities would never be the same. And while the Supreme Court's decision and end of the boycott sparked new threats of reprisals and even violence among some white townspeople, the protesters, the authors claim, could now take their place among the pantheon of American trailblazers. Wilma Dykeman was for many

SOURCE. Wilma Dykeman and James Stokely, "Montgomery Morning," in *The Nation, New York*, January 5, 1957, pp. 355–361. Copyright © 1957 by The Nation Magazine/The Nation Company, Inc. All rights reserved. Reproduced by permission.

years a columnist for the Knoxville, Tennessee, *News Sentinel* and is the author of many books. Her husband, James Stokely, was a business executive and sometime collaborator.

In the still hours just before daylight on the morning of December 21 [1956], fog hung heavy over the dome of Alabama's gleaming white state capitol building. The shrouded streets which stretched away from it through the city of Montgomery were silent. It was easy, in those small hours, to unloose the imagination and wonder if some of the ghosts of 1861 might not be lurking in the "Cradle of the Confederacy" on this morning which was to make Southern history. For if it is true that the hand that rocks the cradle is the hand that rules the world, with a slightly different meaning of words this cradle was presently to be rocked to its foundations.

As daylight came, warm and springlike, Court Square—at the opposite end of the wide main street leading up to the capitol—began to waken. Around the dry fountain, with its tiers of figurines, plump pigeons strutted on the wet pavement. Traffic began to pick up. The giant wreaths of Christmas lights strung across the street became more visible. And the city buses began to roll in and out of the square, loading and unloading passengers. In the doorways of the dress shops, the men's ready-to-wear and hardware stores, the newsstands and the offices and drugstores, people stood watching the buses. This was the morning when a year-old boycott and a generations-old tradition were to end.

A Nervous Morning

Negroes and whites sat or stood at the central segregated bus stop—watching; people drove by slowly, peering from their cars to see what was happening on the buses; and men leaning against the parking meters and standing on the street corners in their shirt sleeves, watched. This was the morning that segregation on the city buses of Montgomery gasped its last and integration breathed its first, and there was tension implied in both the birth and the death.

The morning went quietly. A couple of cars filled with watchful white men in leather jackets parked on two sides of Court Square for the first hour, then slowly moved away. Groups of well-dressed Negro leaders stood at the central bus stop and rode several of the runs. The Rev. Martin Luther King, Jr., who has become the public symbol of the Negro cause, entered a bus and took a seat near the front. The day's pattern developed—most of the buses were only partially filled, but the Negroes rode, for the most part, in the middle seats, a few at the very front, a few at the rear; and the whites rode almost together far to the front. A few whites who were eager for the day to have full meaning rode on the back seat; at least one or two sat by Negroes. By late afternoon the word had gone out over town that "Everything's O.K.; nothing happening."

> 'The real power of the boycott was the Negro women.'

It was the very calmness of the day that was the great news here. People who said nothing had happened meant nothing violent, to make headlines. Actually a great deal had happened which might make news for years to come. Before a new year can begin, an old year must end. Before a new era of human dignity can be born, old indignities must die. On December 21, an era as well as a year came to an end in Montgomery. It was important that Alabamans and Americans alike should realize that what was disappearing was as meaningful as what was developing.

For one thing, the familiar cardboard signs spelling out segregation were gone from the buses. Gone too was the custom that had compelled Negroes to pay their fares at the front door and then often get off the bus and climb back on at the rear door. And the abusive language of some of the drivers calling their passengers "black apes" and "damned n-----s" was stilled. Most apparent of all, perhaps, the stream of walking women had almost disappeared.

"The real power of the boycott was the Negro women," a housewife in one of the white residential areas told us. "Every morning they came by our door here. It was like watching a brook to look out and see them going by steadily for an hour or so every morning and an hour or so every afternoon. And this morning they weren't there. The brook had dried up."

Other things, less tangible but not a whit less real, have gone from Montgomery too. Their essence might be summed up in the words of one Negro: "Now there isn't any more hang-dog looking at a white man. We face him. We got a proud look."

Pride and Humility

On a street in one of the newer residential areas, as we walked along in the pleasant morning between the rows of green lawns and lush pyracantha bushes heavy with clusters of flaming berries, we saw a carload of young schoolboys slow down just past us and shout something before they roared away. We turned and asked a Negro woman walking behind us what they had hollered. Small and lively as a sparrow in her brown coat and brown head-scarf and brown skin, she smiled at us. "They was just meddlin' me. They have to act theyself up. I don't pay them no mind, when they get through actin' theyself up, everything be all right." She had no resentment—against the cruel boys in the present or the bus drivers in the past. "They wasn't all bad. Jus' a few real low mean. My bus driver I hadn' seen in a year welcome me back this mornin'. Like my family I work for: they

25·APR·1959 MACK CHARLES PARKER·TAKEN FROM JAIL AND LYNCHED·POPLARVILLE, MS

24·SEP·1957 PRESIDENT EISENHOWER ORDERS FEDERAL TROOPS TO ENFORCE SCHOOL DESEGREGATION·LITTLE ROCK, AR

···G·1957 CONGRESS PASSES FIRST CIVIL RIGHTS ACT SINCE RECONSTRUCTION

···LIE EDWARDS JR·KILLED BY KLAN ···NTGOMERY, AL

13·NOV·1956 SUPREME COURT BANS SEGREGATED SEATING ON MONTGOMERY BUSES

···1955 MONTGOMERY BUS BOYCOTT BEGINS

DEC·1955 ROSA PARKS ARRESTED FOR REFUSING TO GIVE UP HER SEAT ON BUS TO A WHITE MAN·MONTGOMERY, AL

The Civil Rights Memorial in Montgomery honors the achievements of the era and the memory of those who died. (Jay Sailors/Associated Press.)

told me to stay off the buses, they didn' blame us for what we's doin.'"

We talked with a Negro man who summed up the remarkable self-control his people had shown in this great victory of their boycott. "We don't use the word 'victory,'" he assured us firmly. "We don't want to even have the attitude of the word. Like Reverend King told us at one of our meetings, the attitude of 'victory' wouldn't be worthy of us, and it would be a barrier to the growth we hope for in others."

The conduct and accomplishments of the Negroes during the past year have obviously shaken some of the firmest convictions held by the whites. In the beginning

of the boycott it was often said that Negroes "can't organize anything but a crap game," and if they did, they
"can't hold out." But they did organize, 50,000 strong, and
they didn't develop into an army and they didn't degen-
erate into a mob. They remained individuals united by
a vision. In a region where patience on the long haul is
considered a somewhat less colorful personal asset than
pride in the instant's dramatic gesture, one of the most
astonishing features of this boycott, to white residents,
was the daily plodding persistence with which the Negroes moved toward their goal.

Then, of course, the white people began to admit
the Negroes were organized, but "outsiders" had done
it: Communists, "NAACPs," [chapters of the National
Association for the Advancement of Colored People] . . .
"troublemakers" in general. And, of course, the Negroes
would submit to the old pressures anyway: a few arrests,
some bullying, a few bed-sheets.

"For a while there, the police would stop your car,
maybe two or three times a day," one Negro leader said.
"'Get out, n-----.' You'd show your driving license and
they'd ask you all the questions already filled out on it. Or
they'd book you for going twenty-five miles an hour in a
twenty-mile speed zone."

But the spirit didn't break and the Negroes were
never provoked into retaliation.

Threats and Intimidation

"Then white boys would throw water on us, or a Coca-
Cola bottle from a car. Or once in awhile they'd spit on
us. Even in the last few weeks over twenty cars have had
acid thrown on them."

Mass arrest of the famous ninety was the whites' real
panzer effort at group intimidation that failed and back-
fired. "For the first time," a professor at a local Negro
college told us, "it became honorable to go to jail. Everybody whose name wasn't on that list felt sort of slighted,

like he hadn't done his share." Those who had always been so scared of the police and jail now were clamoring to take the part of the punished.

The final test came when the Ku Klux Klan announced, on the night the Supreme Court handed down its last decision [ending segregation on the buses], that it would stage a demonstration in the Negro part of town. Before such a threat the Negro would once have cowered behind closed doors and darkened windows. But this time the Negro community greeted them almost as it would any other parade. As the estimated forty carloads of Ku Kluxers drove by, lights stayed on, doors were ajar, men, women and children watched openly, in silence. It took enormous courage to face this robed and ancient enemy with such nonchalance. In the end it was the Klan that weakened first. Their parade turned into a side street and disappeared. The Kluxers themselves had set the final seal of solidarity and emancipation on the Negro citizens.

Physical intimidation tailed—and so did economic threats. For if one fact has emerged clearly to both white and Negro community in this crisis it is the intertwining of their economy. As one person put it: "Our schools may not be integrated, but our dollars sure are." Early in the boycott when the Mayor asked the women of Montgomery not to go after their maids and, if the maid wouldn't walk to work, to fire her, one housewife said, "The Mayor can do his own cooking if he wants to. I'm going after my cook." The Negro women knew their employers well enough, too, to be aware of their general distaste for mops and ironing boards. They knew instinctively that these people might tolerate injustice but never inconvenience.

"They talked about firing all the Negroes in the boycott from their jobs," a Negro man told us. "But then I guess they got to thinking about all those white folks' houses we rent. No payroll, no rent. What would those poor white widows living on their husbands' estates do? And what about all those refrigerators and cars and furniture we owed payments on? The storekeepers didn't want that stuff back. They wanted the money. No, after a little thinking there was very few of us fired from work."

A New Understanding of Their Power

Perhaps the most insidious enemy the Negro of Montgomery faced was his attitude toward himself. Indoctrinated for generations by assurances of his inferiority, in many cases he was uncertain as to his own power to sustain this movement. One will tell you now: "I wasn't sure how well we'd stick together or how long we'd last. But the people were way out ahead of the leaders at first. Then we all went together and there wasn't any doubt we'd go on as long as necessary."

> The Negroes have discovered the power of their dollars, the strength of their religion and the hidden resources within themselves.

Under these pressures and doubts, the Negroes have discovered the power of their dollars, the strength of their religion and the hidden resources within themselves. And one of the sorest problems facing Negroes everywhere was met and solved: the bridging of that great gap between the really learned and the desperately illiterate. A white woman in Montgomery who had taken part in interracial group meetings said, "You met time and again with the Negro leaders but somehow you felt that you weren't ever touching the real core—couldn't reach that vast group of Negroes to even know what they were thinking. Even their leaders were isolated from them." But those the Rev. King calls "the Ph.D.'s and the D.s" were brought together by the boycott.

This was true because from first to last the movement worked through the churches. "The only way you can reach the great mass of Southern Negroes today is through their churches," one club woman said, "and the churches were the great power behind the success of this Montgomery boycott. It had religious meaning from the beginning."

Less Despair, More Hope

If there have been improvements in the Negro community of a Sunday, perhaps even more important is the change in the Saturday night world. That cuttings, stabbings and drunkenness have decreased is attested by all the Negroes and admitted by most of the whites. As the pressures of despair and frustration have been partially supplanted by the pressures of self-respect and hopefulness, some of the destructiveness has been supplanted by better citizenship.

> Such calm in the presence of violence must give the whole city pause.

As the first days of bus integration passed without notable incident (a Negro woman reported she was slapped and shoved by a white man as she left the bus, and a white woman on another bus reported that a Negro man winked at her), some of the white community still were far from reconciled. We saw two young men sitting at the bus stop—wild, blue-eyed boys with sun-hardened skins. "Well, Buck, what we gonna do with these damned n-----s?" And one of the leaders of the White Citizens" Council assured us, "The bus situation here is far, far from settled. It can erupt any time. We're doing our best to keep down any violence, but this is a highly charged situation. Some of these boys mean business."

A bulky taxi driver analyzed developments: "It's all looked all right so far. And it may go on quiet enough, if don't nobody get radical. But this thing's touchy. Could be set off any minute. Then who knows what'll happen?"

Another said simply, "The South will always remain the South."

When a shotgun blast was fired at the Rev. King's home on December 23, the pastor did not notify the police. But he mentioned the incident quietly to his congregation during church services. "Even if my attackers 'get' me," he said, "they will still have to 'get' 50,000 other Negroes in Montgomery." He reminded his motionless visitors that "some of us may have to die," but urged his congregation never to falter in the belief that whatever else changed, God's love for all men would continue. "The glory to God that puts man in his place will make brothers of us all," he said. Such calm in the presence of violence must give the whole city pause.

A tentative proposal has been made to start a white bus boycott and organize a white car pool. The illogic of this, in view of the fact that the Negro car pool was ruled illegal a few weeks ago, seems not to have occurred to the proposers. With characteristic Southern humor someone suggested that the Negroes should run an ad in the local paper: "FOR SALE—Slightly used old station wagons for new car pools."!

No matter what may happen tomorrow in Montgomery, the fact remains that the Negro here will never be the same again. What one of the leaders, a tall, dark, articulate man, told us is obviously true: "On December

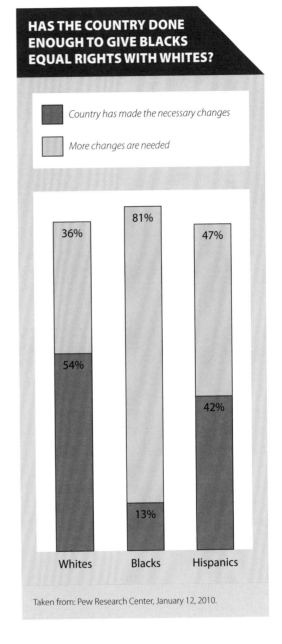

HAS THE COUNTRY DONE ENOUGH TO GIVE BLACKS EQUAL RIGHTS WITH WHITES?

■ Country has made the necessary changes

□ More changes are needed

Whites — 36% / 54%
Blacks — 81% / 13%
Hispanics — 47% / 42%

Taken from: Pew Research Center, January 12, 2010.

5 last year, the Negro in Montgomery grew from a boy to a man. He'll never be the same again. A white man had always said before, 'Boy, go do this,' 'Boy, do that,' and the Negro jumped and did it. Now he says, I don't believe I will,' or he does it, but up straight, looking at the white man. Not a boy any more. He grew up."

The image of the frontiersman has always been vivid in the American mind and memory. One of our frequent laments today is for the disappearing frontier which has been so much a part of American history. To a visitor in Montgomery there is the suggestion of a new frontiersman. His weapons are those of [author Henry David] Thoreau and [Indian independence leader Mohandas] Gandhi rather than [frontiersmen Davy] Crockett and [Daniel] Boone, but the wilderness he faces is no less terrifying. Working on the frontiers of a faith and freedom whose meanings and dynamics have been too little explored before this, these new frontiersmen, black and white, may lead us—and some of the colored and white millions of the world—into a new experience of democracy.

Victory in the Bus Boycott Did Not End Segregation in Montgomery

Randall Kennedy

The end of the Montgomery Bus Boycott did not provide for an easy transition to integration in the city, according to the author of the following selection. Indeed, he argues, white reactions could be loud and sometimes violent while many black people, after the supportive atmosphere of the boycott, hesitated to cross traditional "color lines." Even on the buses, voluntary forms of segregation persisted. Some African Americans returned to old habits of sitting in the back of buses, while some whites stood rather than take available seats. The author notes that in the aftermath of the boycott, Montgomery officials even restated their readiness to maintain segregation in many areas of daily life, even down

---

SOURCE. Randall Kennedy, "Martin Luther King's Constitution: A Legal History of the Montgomery Bus Boycott," *Yale Law Journal*, April, 1989. Copyright © 1989 The Yale Law Journal Company, Inc. All rights reserved. Reproduced by permission of the publisher and author.

to the playing of card games. Randall Kennedy is the Michael R. Klein Professor of Law at Harvard University and the author of four books.

T he Montgomery Bus Boycott has attained a secure and honored niche in the nation's public memory. Indeed, it has become something of a legend. One problem with making legends is that the process engenders a distortive sentimentality. We must thus be careful to prevent admiration for the boycott from exaggerating its accomplishments. The concerted withdrawal of Negro patronage is not what finally desegregated the buses; successful litigation constituted the decisive action. The economic pressure of the boycott forced [bus] company officials to break ranks with the city commissioners. Its moral pressure impelled a few white Montgomerians to commit the apostasy of actually siding with [boycott leader Martin Luther] King. But the boycott on its own did not succeed in inducing the political authorities to make any substantial concessions.

Even within the small social space created by the boycott and its attendant litigation, the transition from segregation was slow and difficult. Browder [the US Supreme Court's *Browder v. Gayle* decision in November 1956] largely stilled official resistance to desegregation aboard local buses. Moreover, many white Montgomerians quietly accepted the new dispensation. But others bitterly and vocally resisted, refusing to sit beside Negroes or in what was formerly the Negro section of buses. An elderly man who stood in the front of a bus despite the presence of vacant seats in the rear spoke for a substantial number of whites when he stated that he 'would rather die and go to hell than sit behind a n-----.' Some die-hards even went so far as to incorporate a private club—the Rebel Club—for the purpose of providing a transportation system available only to whites.

Continuing Resentment

Blacks were often the victims of segregationists' retribution. The evening that the Supreme Court decided Browder, forty carloads of robed and hooded Ku Klux Klansmen rode through Negro neighborhoods honking horns and shining lights into residences. White 'traitors' were targeted as well. The Alabama Association of White Citizens Councils urged 'the real white people of Alabama never to forget the names Rives and Johnson [judges in the original decision in *Browder v. Gayle*].' The judges were deluged with threatening calls and letters. A cross was burned on Judge Johnson's lawn and the gravesite of Judge Rives' son was desecrated.

Segregationist resentment expressed itself in other potentially lethal forms. Two days after the inauguration of desegregated seating, someone fired a shotgun through the front door of King's home. A day later, on Christmas eve [1956], white men attacked a black teenager as she exited a bus. Four days after that, two buses were fired upon by snipers. In one sniper incident, a pregnant woman was shot in both legs. Then, on January 10, 1957, bombs destroyed five black churches and the home of Reverend Robert S. Graetz, one of the few white Montgomerians who had publicly sided with the MIA [Montgomery Improvement Association].

> In practically every other setting, Montgomery remained overwhelmingly segregated.

The City Commission suspended bus service for several weeks on account of the violence. When the violence subsided and service was restored, many black Montgomerians enjoyed their newly recognized right only abstractly; they avoided the anxiety-producing friction that attended what the segregationists called 'race mixing.' The boycott had involved communal withdrawal from the presence of the color line. But for a black rider actually to cross the color line was a different

Freedom Riders used the "colored waiting room" after the boycott, as segregation continued in Montgomery and throughout the South. **(Paul Schutzer/ Contributor/Time & Life Pictures/Getty Images.)**

matter that involved an exercise of individual will and personal vulnerability that for many proved immensely and understandably daunting. For others, the problem involved a loss of that heightened sense of duty which, during the protest, had generated such glorious departures from normalcy. In the aftermath of the boycott the gravitational pull of old habits exerted their force: 'When we first started getting back on the buses I sat up front,' one former boycotter recalled, 'but then I began sitting in the back—I wasn't afraid or nothing: it's just that I was accustomed to it.'

Segregation off the Buses Continues

To the extent that the color line was crossed, the breach extended only to the buses. In practically every other setting, Montgomery remained overwhelmingly segregated, largely because of the popularity (among whites) of sentiments like those expressed by Mayor [W.A.] Gayle when he stated in response to the decision bearing his name:

> The recent Supreme Court decisions . . . have seriously lowered the dignified relations which did exist between the races in our city and in our state. . . . The difficulties [which the invalidated laws were] meant to prevent and the dignities which they guard are not changed here in Alabama by decisions of the Supreme Court. . . . To insure public safety, to protect the peoples of both races, and to promote order in our city we shall continue to enforce segregation.

Underscoring their commitment to the old order, the city commissioners adopted, on March 19, 1957, a city ordinance declaring it:

> unlawful for white and colored persons to play together, or, in company with each other . . . in any game of cards, dice, dominoes, checkers, pool, billiards, softball, basketball, baseball, football, golf, track, and at swimming pools, beaches, lakes or ponds or any other game or games or athletic contests, either indoors or outdoors.

In the early 1960's, Montgomery began formally to rescind such laws, but even that sometimes failed to deprive them of their power. In March 1960, one week after Montgomery rescinded its ordinance requiring segregation in restaurants, ten white college students from Illinois, their professor and his wife, and four Negroes associated with the MIA were arrested in a black-owned restaurant merely for eating together and talking with one another.

The Montgomery Bus Boycott Continues to Inspire Nonviolent Protests Around the World

Hazel Trice Edney

In early 2011, Egyptians flocked into the streets of their cities and engaged in weeks of protest. Their efforts, which were almost entirely nonviolent, helped to bring about the resignation of Hosni Mubarak, who had ruled the country for thirty years. In the following piece, a journalist reports that the Egyptians were partly inspired by the Montgomery Bus Boycott. She asserts that the story of the boycott, including the efforts of Rosa Parks and Martin Luther King Jr., reached Egyptian streets via an Arabic-language translation of a comic-book version of the boycott that originally appeared in 1958. The author goes on to cite the support of African American officials and activists for the events in Egypt. Hazel Trice Edney has been a prominent African American writer for nearly three decades and is the recipient of a career achievement award from New America Media.

Freedom! As the word rang across the airwaves last week from the now famous Tahrir "Liberation" Square in Egypt, Americans—especially African-Americans—readily identified with the passion of the Egyptian people.

For those who witnessed their victory after little more than two weeks of protest, words were difficult to find. Yet, empathy was the overwhelming emotion given the experience of the American civil rights movement, during which the struggle was much greater and much longer.

"As Martin Luther King said in celebrating the birth of a new nation in Ghana while trying to perfect his own, 'There is something in the soul that cries out for freedom.' Those were the cries that came from Tahrir Square, and the entire world has taken note," said President Barack Obama on Feb. 11 [2011] after the announcement that 30-year Egyptian President Hosni Mubarak had resigned in response to the will of the Egyptian people.

Standing Up for Liberation

"The word Tahrir means liberation. It is a word that speaks to that something in our souls that cries out for freedom. And forevermore it will remind us of the Egyptian people—of what they did, of the things that they stood for, and how they changed their country, and in doing so changed the world," Obama said. "Today belongs to the people of Egypt, and the American people are moved by these scenes in Cairo and across Egypt

YOUNG PEOPLE MAKING A DIFFERENCE IN THE MIDDLE EAST

Percentage of young Arabs who answered "yes" to the question, "In your opinion, can [young men or young women] help your country make substantial progress in the next ten years?"

Country	Young men	Young women
Algeria	99%	89%
Jordan	96%	78%
Morocco	96%	79%
Iraq	95%	92%
Tunisia	94%	89%
Egypt	90%	71%
Lebanon	89%	86%
Syria	71%	66%
Libya	66%	55%

Note: Surveys conducted between January and October 2010.

Taken from: Gallup.

because of who we are as a people and the kind of world that we want our children to grow up in."

Congratulatory statements were issued from civil rights leaders around the country, including from Martin Luther King III, president of the Martin Luther King, Jr. Center for Nonviolent Social Change.

"I join with people of good will everywhere in saluting the courageous Egyptians who participated in the nonviolent movement which has brought an end to the Mubarak dictatorship," King said. "Your movement provides an inspiring, visionary example of disciplined nonviolent resistance to oppression, and my prayers and the prayers of people of good will all over the world are with you as you strive to create a vibrant democracy in Egypt."

Widespread reports actually credited the American Civil Rights Movement, particularly the 13-month 1955–1956 Montgomery, Ala., Bus Boycott, for laying the blue print for the success in Egypt. One website, Comicsalliance.com, credits a comic book, first published in 1958 by a non-violent advocacy group, the Fellowship of Reconciliation.

The Story of Montgomery Reaches Egypt

According to *Time* magazine, the comic book, titled, "The Montgomery Story," was recently translated into Arabic by an Egyptian activist named Dalia Ziada, director of the American Islamic Congress. The book, which tells the story of the stance of heroine Rosa Parks and the leadership of Dr. Martin Luther King Jr., was distributed to thousands as a template for non-violent protest.

> An icon of the Civil Rights Movement . . . described the Egyptian movement as 'nothing short of a non-violent revolution.'

"To promote civil disobedience, Ziada last year translated into Arabic a comic-book history about Martin Luther King Jr. and distributed 2,000 copies from Morocco to Yemen," said a *Time* magazine article published March 19, 2009.

U.S. Rep. John Lewis, an icon of the Civil Rights Movement, and a victim of violent police, described the Egyptian movement as "nothing short of a non-violent revolution."

Lewis said in a statement, "The peacefulness of this transition on the streets of Cairo is a testament to the people of Egypt—to the discipline of the protestors and the military—who resisted any temptation to descend into

Many argue that the civil rights movement, and the Montgomery Bus Boycott in particular, inspired pro-democracy protests in Egypt in 2011. (Pedro Ugarte/ AFP/Getty Images.)

brutality. They demonstrated so eloquently the power of peace to persistently broadcast their message of change."

Lewis continued, "Especially this nation which found its own beginnings in a revolutionary movement, we must always try to find ourselves on the just side of budding movements of non-violent change. We must always give credence to any effort that leads to a more truly democratic world society that values the dignity and the worth of every human being. We must always nurture and empower movements which respect freedom of the press, freedom of worship, freedom of assembly, and the inalienable right to dissent."

As the transition began this week, the Egyptian military, an ally of the American military, announced on Sunday that it had dissolved Parliament and the Egyptian constitution as it has been known. The tensions are high because of the unknown future, but the Egyptian military is seen as a friend of the Egyptian people and is expected to work with civilians toward building a democracy.

Understanding the Fight for Equality

Congressional Black Caucus Chairman Emanuel Cleaver II (D-Mo.) recalled the diversity of people who stood for the quick change and the empathy of American people as they watched.

"For nearly three weeks we have watched with baited breath as Egyptians took control of their political destiny. Young and old, rich and poor, religious and secular, men and women flooded the streets demanding their voices be heard," he recalled. "As the Congressional Black Caucus we understand the fight for freedom and equality, as well as the hard work that ensues to build a better future."

The reform in Egypt, which has just begun, will be tedious but can and must be done, reminds Obama.

"By stepping down, President Mubarak responded to the Egyptian people's hunger for change. But this is not the end of Egypt's transition. It's a beginning," President Obama said. "I'm sure there will be difficult days ahead, and many questions remain unanswered. But I am confident that the people of Egypt can find the answers, and do so peacefully, constructively, and in the spirit of unity that has defined these last few weeks. For Egyptians have made it clear that nothing less than genuine democracy will carry the day."

CHAPTER 3

Personal Narratives

Rosa Parks Recalls the Day She Became Defiant

Rosa Parks with Jim Haskins

The following selection is from Rosa Parks's 1992 autobiography. In it Parks remembers the evening when, after a long day at work, she refused to give up her seat on a city bus to a white man. African Americans like Parks were supposed to abandon their seats in the middle of buses if there were white customers to fill them, but that day she refused. The bus driver, a man with whom Parks had had an earlier confrontation, and city policemen ensured that she was taken into custody and jailed at Montgomery City Hall. As soon as she was able, Parks remembers, she phoned her husband to come arrange for her bail and take her home. But by then news of her arrest had reached E.D. Nixon, a local civil rights leader, and Clifford Durr, a white lawyer involved in civil rights. After bail was posted and a trial date set, Parks, her husband, and others went to the Parks's home. There they discussed whether Rosa Parks might be willing to be the plaintiff in a test case challenging segregation on Montgomery's buses.

Photo on previous page: Three thousand people attend a meeting at a church and pledge to continue the five-month-old bus boycott. Mass meetings like this one helped maintain momentum and community pride in the movement. (**Robert W. Kelley/Time & Life Pictures/Getty Images.**)

SOURCE. Rosa Parks with Jim Haskins, "You're Under Arrest," *Rosa Parks: My Story*. New York, NY: Dial Books, 1992, pp. 113–116, 121–124. Copyright © 1992 by Rosa Parks. All rights reserved. Used by permission of Penguin Group (USA) Inc.

When I got off from work that evening of December 1 [1955], I went to Court Square as usual to catch the Cleveland Avenue bus home. I didn't look to see who was driving when I got on, and by the time I recognized him, I had already paid my fare. It was the same driver who had put me off the bus back in 1943, twelve years earlier. He was still tall and heavy, with red, rough-looking skin. And he was still mean-looking. I didn't know if he had been on that route before—they switched the drivers around sometimes. I do know that most of the time if I saw him on a bus, I wouldn't get on it.

I saw a vacant seat in the middle section of the bus and took it. I didn't even question why there was a vacant seat even though there were quite a few people standing in the back. If I had thought about it at all, I would probably have figured maybe someone saw me get on and did not take the seat but left it vacant for me. There was a man sitting next to the window and two women across the aisle.

The next stop was the Empire Theater, and some whites got on. They filled up the white seats, and one man was left standing. The driver looked back and noticed the man standing. Then he looked back at us. He said, "Let me have those front seats," because they were the front seats of the black section. Didn't anybody move. We just sat right where we were, the four of us. Then he spoke a second time: "Y'all better make it light on yourselves and let me have those seats."

The man in the window seat next to me stood up, and I moved to let him pass by me, and then I looked across the aisle and saw that the two women were also standing. I moved over to the window seat. I could not see how standing up was going to "make it light" for

> The more we gave in and complied, the worse they treated us.

me. The more we gave in and complied, the worse they treated us.

I thought back to the time when I used to sit up all night and didn't sleep, and my grandfather would have his gun right by the fireplace, or if he had his one-horse wagon going anywhere, he always had his gun in the back of the wagon. People always say that I didn't give up my seat because I was tired, but that isn't true. I was not tired physically, or no more tired than I usually was at the end of a working day. I was not old, although some people have an image of me as being old then. I was forty-two. No, the only tired I was, was tired of giving in.

The driver of the bus saw me still sitting there, and he asked was I going to stand up. I said, "No." He said, "Well, I'm going to have you arrested." Then I said, "You may do that." These were the only words we said to each other. I didn't even know his name, which was James Blake, until we were in court together. He got out of the bus and stayed outside for a few minutes, waiting for the police.

As I sat there, I tried not to think about what might happen. I knew that anything was possible. I could be manhandled or beaten. I could be arrested. People have asked me if it occurred to me then that I could be the test case the NAACP [National Association for the Advancement of Colored People] had been looking for. I did not think about that at all. In fact if I had let myself think too deeply about what might happen to me, I might have gotten off the bus. But I chose to remain. . . .

Calling from Prison

I called home. My husband and mother were both there. She answered the telephone. I said, "I'm in jail. See if Parks [her husband Raymond] will come down here and get me out."

She wanted to know, "Did they beat you?"

I said, "No, I wasn't beaten, but I am in jail."

She handed him the telephone, and I said, "Parks, will you come get me out of jail?"

He said, "I'll be there in a few minutes." He didn't have a car, so I knew it would be longer. But while we were still on the phone, a friend came by in his car. He'd heard about my being in jail and had driven to our place on Cleveland Court to see if he could help. He said he'd drive Parks to the jail.

The matron then took me back to the cell.

As Parks' friend had indicated, the word was already out about my arrest. Mr. [E.D.] Nixon had been notified by his wife, who was told by a neighbor, Bertha Butler, who had seen me escorted off the bus. Mr. Nixon called the jail to find out what the charge was, but they wouldn't tell him. Then he had tried to reach Fred Gray, one of the two black lawyers in Montgomery, but he wasn't home. So finally Mr. Nixon called Clifford Durr, the white lawyer who was [white civil rights activist and friend] Mrs. Virginia Durr's husband. Mr. Durr called the jail and found out that I'd been arrested under the segregation laws. He also found out what the bail was.

Meanwhile Parks had called a white man he knew who could raise the bail. His friend took him over to the man's house to pick him up. I don't remember how much the bail was.

When I got back to the cell, [a cellmate] had found some little crumpled-up paper, and she wrote both of her brothers' names and telephone numbers on it. She said to call them early in the morning because they went to work around six A.M. I told her I would.

Just then the matron came to let me know that I was being released, and the woman hadn't given me the piece of paper. They were rushing me out, and she was right behind me. She knew she would not get through the iron-mesh door at the end of the stairs, so she threw it down the stairs and it landed right in front of me. I picked it up and put it in my pocket.

Mrs. Durr was the first person I saw as I came through the iron mesh door with matrons on either side of me. There were tears in her eyes, and she seemed shaken, probably wondering what they had done to me. As soon as they released me, she put her arms around me, and hugged and kissed me as if we were sisters.

I was real glad to see Mr. Nixon and Attorney Durr too. We went to the desk, where I picked up my personal belongings and was given a trial date. Mr. Nixon asked that the date be the following Monday, December 5, 1955, explaining that he was a Pullman porter [a railway employee] and would be out of Montgomery until then. We left without very much conversation, but it was an emotional moment. I didn't realize how much being in jail had upset me until I got out.

As we were going down the stairs, Parks and his friends were driving up, so I got in the car with them, and Mr. Nixon followed us home.

Finally Back Home

By the time I got home, it was about nine-thirty or ten at night. My mother was glad to have me home and wanted to know what she could do to make me comfortable. I told her I was hungry (for some reason I had missed lunch that day), and she prepared some food for me. Mrs. Durr and my friend Bertha Butler were there, and they helped my mother. I was thinking about having to go to work the next day, but I knew I would not get to bed anytime soon.

> I knew that I would never, never ride another segregated bus, even if I had to walk to work.

Everyone was angry about what had happened to me and talking about how it should never happen again. I knew that I would never, never ride another segregated bus, even if I had to walk to work. But it still had not occurred to me that mine could be a test case against the segregated buses.

Then Mr. Nixon asked if I would be willing to make my case a test case against segregation. I told him I'd have to talk with my mother and husband. Parks was pretty angry. He thought it would be as difficult to get people to support me as a test case as it had been to develop a test case out of Claudette Colvin's experience [another instance of a woman who refused to give up her Montgomery bus seat in the spring of 1955]. We discussed and debated the question for a while. In the end Parks and my mother supported the idea. They were against segregation and were willing to fight it. And I had worked on enough cases to know that a ruling could not be made without a plaintiff. So I agreed to be the plaintiff.

A Montgomery Bus Boycott Leader Remembers Its Inspirations and Challenges

Ralph David Abernathy

Ralph David Abernathy, the author of the following selection, was a major civil rights leader and a close friend and colleague of Martin Luther King Jr. He was also one of the leading figures in the Montgomery Bus Boycott. In 1955, Abernathy was a pastor at the First Baptist Church in Montgomery, one of the oldest and largest African American churches in the South. For his part, King had in 1954 become a pastor at the Dexter Avenue Baptist Church in Montgomery, moving there from his home in Atlanta, Georgia. Pastors like Abernathy and King, and Reverends Powell and Huffman of the Holt Street Baptist Church, held positions of status and authority in Montgomery's African American community. Abernathy's account begins when, on December 5, 1955, he and King drove to the Holt Street Church to attend a meeting on whether to extend the bus boycott begun that same day. They were surprised to find thousands of people waiting, ready to commit themselves to a longer protest. Abernathy also recalls how King argued that the protesters must use only the methods of nonviolent, passive resistance, and how such methods not only succeeded but became the heart of a much wider civil rights effort. The leaders of the boycott, Abernathy remembers, had to struggle to maintain the momentum of the boycott in the face of legal challenges and violence.

That evening [December 5, 1955] I picked up Martin [Luther King Jr.], and though we had thus far accomplished everything we'd set out to do, there was still one more question to answer: even though our people had stayed off the buses all day (we spotted fewer than ten), would they turn out in force tonight? We were certain most blacks knew about the meeting, and we knew many would come, but Holt Street Baptist Church held one thousand people, and even if five hundred showed, people would still say the meeting was a failure, since we didn't fill up the church.

As we drove through the darkened streets we told each other the people would turn out, but we didn't really believe it. About five blocks away from the church we saw cars parked on both sides of the street; and when we were about three blocks away, the driveways and front yards were also filled up. First we thought it was a party, then Martin and I came to the same conclusion simultaneously—somebody extremely important had died, the head deacon or the preacher himself.

> They were crying out of a sense of newfound freedom, not cheering us so much as cheering themselves for what they had done that day.

Surprising Mass Support

I turned at the next corner and drove away from the church until I finally found a space and parked. When we got out we heard the first sound—a low growl somewhere in the distance. It took a moment before we realized that what we heard was a huge crowd of people, not shouting or cheering the way they do in a football stadium, but talking among themselves. I think at that moment, I realized what it was, and I felt my spine tingle.

When we rounded the last corner we saw them, milling in the dark shadows of the overhanging oaks—hordes of people, a whole army of them, more people than I had ever seen in my life. As my eyes scanned the horizon in both directions all I saw was the crowd. It seemed to spill into the next neighborhood on all sides. The church yard was literally too small to contain them all. Someone who made an effort to count them said there were more than four thousand in the church yard and another thousand inside.

I heard Martin mutter something under his breath, an expression of surprise. As we approached someone saw us and called out, then they all turned toward us and began to make a pathway for us to pass through.

Then the crowd started applauding, politely at first, then louder and louder. Finally they were applauding wildly and cheering. The mayor and his two commissioners must have heard that whoop clear over on the other side of town. When we entered the church the noise was magnified ten times. They were crying out of a sense of newfound freedom, not cheering us so much as cheering themselves for what they had done that day, what we had all done. I don't think I have ever heard a more joyous sound in my life, and as I looked over at Martin I knew he felt the same extraordinary sense of unity among our people. At that moment we both knew that we were on the brink of a great victory, though how great and how costly we could not at that moment have imagined.

The crowd applauded and cheered for fifteen minutes. We stood there, smiling and waving, then Martin signaled for order. But a lifetime of pent-up emotions had been released and the people were enjoying their new-found freedom. So we waited until the crowd had finally shouted and screamed enough. Then, as presiding officer, I motioned for them to be seated. At that moment complete silence settled on the church, and outside the loud mumbling also ceased. You could have heard a dog bark on the other side of town.

Then I called for Gladys Black, the outstanding minister of music at Holt Street Church, to lead us in "What a Fellowship, What a Joy Divine," which became the first hymn to be used in the new movement. Everyone knew it by heart, and since it had no revolutionary overtones, we could always sing it publicly without fear of suspicion or criticism. So the crowd rocked the rafters.

> If one small group (or even a single individual) struck back with fist or club or gun then we would lose the moral advantage we were striving to achieve.

At some point—probably when they saw the size of the crowd—Reverends Powell and Huffman, who had told me they were too ill to read the lesson and lead us in prayer, experienced miraculous cures. The scales fell from Powell's eyes and he was able to open the meeting with a lengthy reading of the scripture. Huffman's laryngitis had disappeared and he was able to recite a long and remarkably resonant prayer. These were the first of many miracles that would occur over the next fifteen years, the proof that God helps those who have the will and courage to help themselves.

Then, because I was better known, I introduced Martin to the crowd, and he stepped forward and began to speak. He recited the now familiar story of Mrs. Parks's arrest. Then he explained what had happened at the afternoon meeting—the formation of the new organization and its slate of officers. Again spontaneous applause and shouting broke out, and we could hear the crowd outside joining in, even though few could understand every word over the primitive loudspeaker system that Reverend Wilson had hurriedly put in place. In a few weeks there would be many more audiences like this one outside, all over the country, not physically present in the churches where we held our mass meetings and demonstrations, but cheering us on just the same as they heard the words over radios or occasionally saw our black-and-white images on television screens.

Training in Nonviolence

What happened after Martin had finished his report about the afternoon meeting was crucial to the success of the Montgomery bus boycott and, on a larger scale, the civil rights movement itself: After talking about the new developments in the Supreme Court, developments that would soon pave the way for racial equality, he began to explain in careful detail the theory of nonviolent protest. I'm sure no white person in Montgomery that night could have dreamed that a thousand blacks—many of them uneducated, some illiterate—were sitting quietly in a church while one of their preachers lectured to them on Henry David Thoreau and Mahatma Gandhi [earlier advocates of nonviolence]. Yet that is precisely what Martin did—and at some length.

That lesson was crucial. We were asking these people to go into the streets and to accept whatever punishment the white community had to offer, whether jail or beating or death; and we were asking them to take this risk *without ever raising a hand in their own defense.* So it was only fair that they understand thoroughly why they were being asked to do something so contrary to human nature. The success of this strategy depended on every single person in the black community reacting in precisely the same way. If one small group (or even a single individual) struck back with fist or club or gun then we would lose the moral advantage we were striving to achieve. It was absolutely essential that the decent people in the community, as well as in the nation at large, see Jim Crow [southern laws segregating blacks and whites] for what it really was—an oppressive system maintained by the persistent threat of violence. It was that violence we wanted to expose. For only when it came out from behind the mask of legalism and respectability could people of good will fully understand our predicament and act to free us. This is the lesson Martin taught that night.

To be more precise, that is the lesson he *began* to teach, because nonviolence wasn't just a technique you learned in a single evening. It was a habit of mind, a way of life that had to be learned slowly and thoroughly. It was not just one lesson but an entire curriculum, and this was the first of many lectures that Martin gave to these same people—at least twice a week for the next year, and sometimes three and four times a week. Later we introduced Saturday workshops in nonviolence during which people would undergo simulated attacks, both verbal and physical, learning how to be silent in the face of shouts of abuse and how to fall limp in the arms of arresting policemen. These workshops became a regular part of our training programs in Birmingham, Selma, Chicago, and Mississippi. It was the philosophical groundwork for these workshops that Martin began to lay on that very first night.

Committing to the Boycott's Hardships

Unbeknownst to us, we were also creating the format for later meetings. After Martin had finished with his speech on nonviolence, I stepped forward to read a resolution calling for all blacks to stay off the buses until the white establishment had acceded to our demands. Now the chips were on the table. We were asking them to suffer substantial inconvenience in order to bring about a modest change in procedures and had they chosen to balk, we would have closed down the show and gone home.

But of course that didn't happen. When I asked them if they supported the resolution, they came to their feet, shouting their willingness to go forward with the plan. It was a glorious moment, the single instant in which we knew they had committed themselves wholeheartedly to our leadership. Although from time to time they experienced doubts and faltered briefly, they never really turned from the purpose to which they committed themselves that night. And in the final analysis, it was their commitment that ensured our final victory.

This first meeting was so successful that we repeated the same format in future rallies, both in Montgomery and elsewhere. We would begin with scripture, prayer, and perhaps a hymn. Then Martin would talk about the abuses we were facing, the remedies we proposed, and the way in which nonviolent protest would accomplish our ends. Usually other leaders would follow Martin in saying a few words. Sometimes we would have a guest "pep speaker" from another city. But I would almost always close out the meeting with a plea to "stay off the buses" or "meet at such-and-such a church" or "be sure not to resist when you are arrested"—whatever practical advice was needed to put the current plan into operation. So the meeting would begin with the enunciation of principles and broad strategy and would end with attention to particular tactics. As program chairman, I was in charge of tactics.

We closed the meeting that night with a rousing hymn, and the huge church trembled from the vibrations. Later I wondered what the white sheriff's deputies must have thought, parked a block away, hunched down in their cars, ordered to report everything they saw and heard. The sight of five thousand blacks in attendance must have impressed them, but the sound of our cheers and singing must have unnerved them even more.

The only question left to answer, both for them and for us, was: How long could we keep it up?

The next day Martin met with the press and made our position quite clear. We would end the boycott only when our demands were granted, which were reasonable and should pose no problems for local authorities.

"We are not asking for an end to segregation. That's a matter for the legislature and the courts," he was quoted as saying. "We feel that we have a plan within the law. All we are seeking is justice and fair treatment in riding the buses. We don't like the idea of Negroes having to stand when there are vacant seats. We are demanding justice on that point."

> It is important to note the modest nature of our demands and the reasonable tone in which they were spoken.

It is important to note the modest nature of our demands and the reasonable tone in which they were spoken. At this stage we were not breaking current law, at least not to our knowledge. (Later an obscure labor statute would be used to intimidate us.) In fact, we were merely calling for "justice" under current law, which prescribed that we could not be driven from our seats unless other places were available. We were not even asking that the buses be desegregated—only that a more acceptable form of segregation be adopted, one used throughout the state and region.

Digging in on the Boycott

After the first month, the struggle ceased to be a series of attacks and counterattacks and became trench warfare—a prolonged confrontation that required a special kind of character in order to survive and achieve victory. For Martin and me it meant the daily revitalizing of our people's will to stay off the city buses and—despite the inconvenience—to make alternative arrangements to get to work. At the beginning this was an easier task because

Mrs. Parks's case was fresh in everybody's mind and because it was something of an adventure. In addition, the national press gave us increasing attention. We saw the story of our struggle move to the front page of the *New York Times*, and after that to the front pages of newspapers throughout the country. As long as we were a major item it was easy to hold our ranks and continue to march to and from work every morning and every night.

But very soon the press lost interest in our daily routine. A story with no new developments is no story at all. And when our struggle was not being carried on the Associated Press wires, the nation forgot about us. The torrent of telegrams and letters slowed to a trickle and then stopped altogether. It became increasingly difficult for us to keep our people's spirits from flagging, even with Sunday sermons and Wednesday prayers. With daily urging by local whites to give up the struggle, some blacks were longing to return to the peace of years gone by, even if it was a peace without dignity or hope. As days became weeks, morale was more and more the central concern of the black leadership.

By the same token, the white leadership was not having an easy time either. The bus line was losing money and one route after another was dropped in order to cut losses to a minimum. The parent company in Chicago was unhappy, and they blamed the local politicians for an unmanageable mess that the Cook County machine would never have permitted.

As for the white politicians, in their frustration they were beginning to go for one another's throats. The more reasonable among them, not a large group, were pushing for an accommodation with us, one that would give us some of what we wanted. The racist-populist element was hoping to ride to power on a new surge of anti-black sentiment, a viewpoint already being exploited by citizens councils throughout the South. Several politicians were leading the Alabama Citizens Council, and while their public statements were politely and peaceably racist, in private most were saying that they were prepared, if necessary, to use violence, just as their fathers and grandfathers had done to keep us in our place. . . .

For a while the white establishment bided its time, assuming that eventually we would weary of the daily chore of walking to work and come trudging by twos and threes back to the bus line. We worried about that possibility as well, and very early in the game we decided to create our own transportation system.

Organizing Carpools

We immediately organized a car pool to help those people in the greatest need—those who lived a great distance from town and who could walk to work and to shop only with great difficulty. Soon we established regular pick-up stops, where people could stand and be certain that when another black drove past, he or she would stop and take on passengers. Later, when we began to receive contributions from around the country, we decided to buy a fleet of station wagons, enough so that each church could have one. Then we would run a free service for all who needed a ride. We would establish regular routes with a regular schedule and then adapt to special needs and circumstances. Our ultimate goal: That no one in the black community should suffer because of the boycott.

> We decided to buy a fleet of station wagons, enough so that each church could have one.

It took us a while to collect enough money, but we made our needs known to blacks and sympathetic whites throughout the nation and, in a shorter time than we could have hoped, we had gathered enough to buy the wagons. Each church had a different color. Ours was red, because that was my favorite.

Needless to say, when the whites saw us inaugurate our free service, they were infuriated. It was something

Contributions from all over the country helped finance a fleet of station wagons to transport people during the boycott. (Don Cravens/ Contributor/Time & Life Pictures/Getty Images.)

they hadn't anticipated, if for no other reason than because of the expense involved. They were used to seeing blacks driving around in ten-year-old Buicks, not in brand-new Ford wagons. For several weeks they fumed.

Their morale was further weakened by the report of the bus company after the first of the year: they were losing twenty-two cents per mile under current conditions, even with routes curtailed or eliminated. At that rate they would soon be out of business. With no relief in sight, they asked for an increase in the fare—from ten to twenty cents. That amount seems paltry by today's standards, but in 1956 it was not an irrelevant sum to people living on marginal incomes, white as well as black. And since by then the boycott was virtually 100 percent effective, that meant the increase in fare was going to be borne by whites.

At this point things turned ugly. We began to get threatening phone calls, many of them obscene. Virtually every one of MIA's [Montgomery Improvement Association] known leaders received such calls; and no matter how often you told your wife that anyone making anonymous threats would be too cowardly to carry them out, you never quite convinced her or yourself. You knew that in the past blacks had been gunned down from cover of darkness or else dragged to obscure wooded areas by masked men and then lynched. So violence was always a very real possibility, even when your demands were modest and expressed in the most moderate of terms.

A White Minister Remembers the Beginning of the Montgomery Bus Boycott

Robert S. Graetz

In the following selection, a white resident of Montgomery, Alabama, recalls his sympathy for and choice to participate in the Montgomery Bus Boycott. In 1955, Robert S. Graetz was a pastor at Montgomery's Trinity Lutheran Church, which had a mostly African American congregation. Some church members made it known on Sunday, December 4, 1955, that there was a planned boycott of the city's buses to take place the next day. As Graetz writes, he and his wife decided not only to be involved in that Monday's event, but to continue their participation when the

SOURCE. Robert S. Graetz, *Montgomery: A White Preacher's Memoir*. Minneapolis: Fortress Press, 1991, 44–52. All rights reserved. Reproduced by permission of New South Books.

boycott turned into a mass protest at the large meeting held at Holt Street Baptist Church that evening. Graetz and his family suffered for their choice, facing disdain and hatred from other white citizens of Montgomery. Pastor Robert S. Graetz continues to serve a congregation in Ohio and remains active in civil rights.

With the boycott imminent, Jeannie [Graetz's wife] and I had a decision to make. I had promised our church officials that I would concentrate on being a pastor and would not start trouble. I did not want to violate the spirit of my agreement, so in response to this call for action, we sought God's guidance. During the rest of that day, we prayed off and on, asking God what our role should be and what I should say to our congregation on Sunday morning.

Soon the answer was clear. We had to be involved. Afterward, we realized that if we had remained aloof, our effectiveness in the Negro community would have disintegrated. We would have had to pack up and move out. Though we realized that our decision put our entire family in danger, we intended to do whatever our Lord told us.

> We had not only taken residence among the Negro people of Montgomery, but from that point on, their struggle became our own.

Sunday morning the people who gathered at Trinity Lutheran Church shared the emotions experienced in churches all over town. I'm sure my announcement echoed dozens of others.

"As you no doubt know, Mrs. Rosa Parks was arrested on Thursday for refusing to give up her seat on a city bus to a white man. The Negro leaders of Montgomery have called for a boycott of the buses tomorrow to protest her arrest and the bad treatment of many people on the buses. I am appealing to every one of you to take part in this boycott. Share the ride tomorrow. I will be out with my car early in the morning, driving people to work. Jeannie will be by the phone at home. If you need a ride, please call.

"Let's try to make this boycott as effective as possible because it won't be any boycott if half of us ride the buses and half don't ride. So if we're going to do it, let's make a good job of it."

Joining the Protest

There was no turning back for us. We had not only taken residence among the Negro people of Montgomery, but from that point on, their struggle became our own.

That weekend a minor event played a key role in the success of the boycott. A Negro maid who had received one of the flyers asked her employer if she might have Monday off. When asked why, the maid brought out the flyer and showed it to her.

The white woman was shocked but pleased at the opportunity to undercut the plans of the "colored" people. "You can have Monday off if you let me have that paper," she said.

The employer hurried to the office of the *Montgomery Advertiser* and headed for the desk of Joe Azbell, City Editor. "Look at this," she cried.

Instantly Joe had a front-page story for Sunday's paper. The headline read: "Negroes to Boycott Buses Monday." Joe Azbell's straightforward article reported the arrest of Mrs. Parks, the proposed one-day boycott, and the meeting planned for Monday evening. He would cover the meeting himself.

As the news spread over the weekend, many of Montgomery's Negroes doubted whether the boycott would work. Such plans had been talked about for years with no results. Even Dr. [Martin Luther] King and the other leaders experienced misgivings about how their people would respond.

But excitement grew as Negroes in home after home picked up their papers from their porches on Sunday morning and read the front-page story. "I guess it really *is* going to happen," they said. . . .

As I cruised the streets that Monday morning [December 5, 1955], I saw Negro people striding along as if they didn't have a care in the world, their heads held high, their faces covered with smiles. They seemed unconcerned about whether they walked or rode. What they were doing was more important than how or when they reached their destination. I had never seen such proud, confident, happy people.

Their message was clear: "We are colored, Negro, black. We are whatever we decide we are. We are people of value and worth. With God's help we will determine our own destiny, no longer allowing white people to push us around as if they owned us. Whatever they may do to us, we will not be afraid."

A New Beginning

A new day had dawned in Montgomery. We didn't know it at the time, but a new day had dawned for America as well. Though many decades before December 5, 1955, many individual Negroes fit this pattern, never before had this spirit been so pervasive.

Another factor contributed to the boycott's success. Rumors spread through the white community that Negro "goon squads" would roam the streets, forcibly keeping people off the buses. To prevent this the police department assigned two motorcycle officers to follow each bus that drove into a Negro neighborhood. According to the *Advertiser* that morning, city officials promised to "call out every city policeman and every reserve policeman, if necessary, to maintain law and order."

A handful of Negro people had decided to ride the buses in spite of the boycott, but most changed their minds when they saw the motorcycles. One potential

rider said, "Look at that! They even have the police out to make sure we don't get on the buses."

The boycott was nearly 100 percent effective, exceeding the wildest dreams of those who had proposed it.

Dr. King said later that he would have considered a 60 percent response a success. But when he and his wife, Coretta, watched the first bus roll by their South Perry Street home, at 6:00 A.M., it was empty!

Mr. Robert Dandridge [an African American parishoner and friend] called us later in the day. "I've been

Rev. Robert Graetz, leader of an African American congregation, chose to participate in the bus boycott despite violence against his family from other white citizens. (Don Cravens/ Contributor/Time & Life Pictures/Getty Images.)

sitting on my porch since early this morning, watching the buses drive by," he said. "And they're as naked as they can be!"

One old man said, "Pastor Graetz, this is the first time our people have stuck together in anything."

That afternoon the *Alabama Journal* reported:

> At 5:30 A.M. today the big yellow busses of the Montgomery City Lines began pulling into Court Square to pick up passengers.

> Generally a swarm of Negro passengers are waiting at the stop for the busses to take them to the railroad shops, private homes, laundries, factories and jobs throughout the city. . . .

> Negroes were on almost every corner in the downtown area, silent, waiting for rides or moving about to keep warm, but few got on busses.

One of the local papers carried a picture of a crudely lettered sign: Remember We Are Fighting for a Cause. Do Not Ride a Bus Today. . . .

I wanted to get to the [December 5, 1955] meeting at Holt Street Baptist Church plenty early. Mr. Dandridge and I planned to go together. (I could always count on him.)

But what a surprise when we arrived at the church! The doorway, the sidewalk, and even the street were filled with people, all Negroes except for some city police officers, as far as I could tell. . . .

The proceedings finally began with a hymn and a prayer. Soon I recognized a voice on the loudspeaker, that of the minister from the Dexter Avenue Baptist Church, Dr. Martin Luther King, Jr. His words galvanized the crowd.

> *We avoided the negative connotations of the term* boycott, *calling our actions a* protest movement.

He talked about what had happened to Mrs. Parks and about the general treatment of Negroes on the buses and elsewhere. As Dr. King discussed the day's activities, he used a word that had not come up before, *protest.*

During the months that we stayed off the buses, we avoided the negative connotations of the term *boycott,* calling our actions a *protest movement.* We were not attempting to penalize the bus company for their past sins, merely protesting injustice.

Dr. King told the crowd that they should not stoop to treating white people the way white people had treated them. He closed by saying, "If you will protest courageously, and yet with dignity and Christian love, when the history books are written in future generations, the historians will have to pause and say, 'There lived a great people—a black people—who injected new meaning and dignity into the veins of civilization.' This is our challenge and our overwhelming responsibility."

I heard those words echoed in many mass meetings after that. Speakers would say, "Let the history books record that there was a people in Montgomery, Alabama—a black people . . ." and the crowd would roar its approval.

After Dr. King's address, Mrs. Parks, sitting in the front row, was introduced. This gentle woman's quiet dignity and courage had inspired fifty-thousand Negroes to stand up for their human rights, to stand together, imbued with their own dignity and courage. And that night they stood together to give her a standing ovation.

Then Rev. Ralph Abernathy presented the only items of business that night. The first question put to the assembly: "Do you want to end the protest and get back on the buses?"

"No, no!" came the resounding chorus.

Ralph then read a resolution including three demands the bus company would have to meet before Montgomery's Negroes would return to the buses:

1. A guarantee of courteous treatment to be given to all passengers.

2. Passengers to be seated on a first-come, first-served basis, with Negroes starting from the back and whites from the front. Wherever the two groups met, the line would be drawn. Negroes would no longer have to give up their seats if additional white passengers got on the bus.

3. Negro drivers to be hired for the routes which went primarily into Negro communities.

The resolution was adopted unanimously.

The mild nature of the demands drew no argument that night. Though Dr. King had talked about the evils of segregation, the resolution asked for only a *change* in the segregated system, not its demise. For that reason the National Association for the Advancement of Colored People [NAACP] at first refused to support the Montgomery protest. Some national NAACP leaders were appalled at our meekness. Ultimately, we realized that our "meekness" was providential.

White leaders responded to our demands by saying they could do nothing about the seating system mandated by law. "If you don't like the law, change it," they said. They knew we couldn't, however, because no Negroes participated in the legislative process at that time. But weeks later, when nothing was done about our mild demands, a suit was filed in federal court, challenging the constitutionality of Alabama's bus segregation law.

One more announcement was made before the mass meeting ended. A new organization called the Montgomery Improvement Association [MIA] had been formed that afternoon to provide leadership for the protest. Dr. Martin Luther King, Jr., had been elected president.

The MIA board faced some incredibly difficult tasks at the start. Not only did they have to negotiate with city and bus company officials. Now that the protest would continue, they also had to develop procedures for getting people to work and to shopping. This movement might last for weeks. It was December. We were heading into the worst of our winter weather.

None of us dreamed that more than a year would pass before the buses would integrate and our protest would end.

"None of us dreamed that more than a year would pass before the buses would integrate and our protest would end.

Volunteering to Drive

The MIA board made transportation and finances top priorities. Negro taxis in Montgomery had given people rides on the first day for ten cents, the same as bus fare, but they could not continue that practice. Our volunteer car pool had also worked well on the first day, but making that work for any length of time required good coordination. The board set up committees to raise money and to establish a regular schedule for the volunteer car pool. Committee members worked almost around the clock for the first week or so.

Our phone rang about 2:00 one morning, and the transportation committee gave me my assignment. They told me the route I was to drive and the hours I should be there. For the next several weeks I drove people to work from 6:00 to 9:00 every morning. Though I had already volunteered, the committee seemed timid about asking me to do much. Others put in many more hours than I did.

Few of the five thousand people at that meeting in the Holt Street Baptist Church thought about practical problems. The vast majority were too intent on celebrating the miracle. Fifty thousand black people had stood against their oppressors, not counting the cost. Proud of what they had begun, they would let nothing turn them back. One of the songs of the movement expressed Montgomery's heart-felt cry: "Ain't gonna let nobody turn me 'round, turn me 'round; I'm headin' for the Freedom Land!"

The meeting now ended, Mr. Dandridge and I slowly moved with the crowd out of the building. Many people greeted Mr. Dandridge. Few knew who I was, so he introduced me to his friends as we inched along.

One man shook my hand and smiled broadly. "Did you enjoy the meeting?" he asked.

"Enjoy it?" snapped Mr. Dandridge. "He's part of it!"

Mr. Dandridge was right. Years before, I had dreamed of pretending I was a Negro to become more involved in the fight for justice. Now I was part of a Negro movement destined to launch the modern civil rights movement in America.

The Montgomery Bus Boycott and Christmas 1955

Jo Ann Gibson Robinson

The author of the following selection was one of the first to advocate a boycott of Montgomery, Alabama's buses. A leading member
of the city's Women's Political Council and a professor at Alabama
State College, Jo Ann Gibson Robinson had, like Rosa Parks and
other women, suffered indignities on the buses from white drivers.
After hearing of Parks's arrest and the plans to respond, she printed thousands of leaflets calling for a one-day boycott on Monday,
December 5, 1955. Once the boycott expanded, she joined the
executive council of the Montgomery Improvement Association,
headed by Martin Luther King Jr., to guide the event. In this viewpoint, she writes of December 1955, when Montgomery's African
Americans were adjusting to the reality of the boycott, including

SOURCE. Jo Ann Gibson Robinson, *The Montgomery Bus Boycott
and the Women Who Started It: The Memoir of Jo Ann Gibson
Robinson*. Knoxville: The University of Tennessee Press, 1987,
pp. 95–100. Copyright © 1987 by The University of Tennessee Press/
Knoxville. All rights reserved. Reproduced by permission.

the likelihood that Christmas celebrations would be limited that year. She notes the effect the boycott had on the city's businesses, because many protesters boycotted certain merchants as well as the buses. But despite increasing tension and suspicion, Gibson writes, people were committed to continuing the fight for equal treatment on the city's transportation system.

During the cold days of December [1955], boycotters walked. The protest, which was to last for one day, had continued. Christmas shopping and heavy packages did not deter blacks from the pledge not to ride the buses again until their demands had been met. Many Christmas shoppers, not waiting for a pickup, walked and carried heavy, cumbersome bundles in their arms, on their backs, or, as one *Life Magazine* photograph showed, on their heads.

At this phase, the Christmas shopping season, the boycott received very little attention from local news media. The period was nonetheless important to boycotters. In addition to the bus boycott itself, many boycotters decided not to buy from merchants or businesses that Christmas.

> Many black Montgomerians decided to purchase only essentials such as food and necessary clothing until the boycott ended.

Rethinking Christmas

First of all, the Montgomery business community had shown little support for the boycott. There had been letters from individuals condemning the inhuman treatment of blacks on bus lines, but not one from any of the corporations who owed so much of their success to black customers. So, individually, many black Montgomerians decided to purchase only essentials such as food and necessary clothing, until the boycott ended. And many decided to trade only with Negro businessmen.

Second, since many boycotters owned no cars and needed buses to reach the big stores in downtown Montgomery, they stayed at home and bought only essentials. Thus, for most of them, toys were out. So were Christmas trees and decorations. There was little or no discarding of faded or tight overcoats, shirts, dresses, or suits. Walking had reduced the sizes of most boycotters, anyway! Also, new furniture some people had planned as a Christmas present to themselves was forgotten. Certainly out of the question was the Christmas replacement of a six-year-old automobile; the old car ran as well as could be expected and was getting them and the boycotters where they wanted to go. If others had promised themselves a renovated home, or the addition of a room, such ideas were cast aside. Following the trend, Negro children learned to make rag dolls and to fix old toys that had been discarded. Passersby could see children playing in their yards with balls that had been taped or wrapped, or with dolls whose heads had been glued on. One child was seen crying on Christmas Day because one of her doll's eyes had dropped down into its head. Her mother promised to fish them out and glue them back on. This seemed to pacify the child, for she stopped crying.

Usually there was eager expectation for festivity at the Yuletide season, but this 1955 Christmas nobody seemed to have the desire to put up Christmas decorations. They did put up those left over from the year before. But, on the whole, people now planned to spend the season more quietly, solemnly, prayerfully. As they vowed to spend less, to learn to save more, and even to sacrifice some things they needed but did not just have to have, black people this year gave no gifts! Friends who were in the habit of exchanging presents asked that the practice be discontinued for this year. Word circulated that all black people should spend the season in meditation and prayer, instead of dancing and entertaining friends.

Thus, black Americans were boycotting the buses intentionally, but boycotting businesses unintentionally. They just were not buying that year. And the more economical they became, the less money the stores took in. According to published reports, one merchant stated that Montgomery's stores took in $2 million less during December 1955 than during previous Christmas seasons.

An Unintentional Contribution to the Boycott

In addition, white bus riders also had trouble with transportation. The Montgomery bus company had operated buses or trolley cars in the city for more than twenty years, and not for one day had those vehicles failed to run their regular routes. But on Thursday, December 22, under the pretext that drivers were entitled to holidays, the bus company ran the following paid advertisement in the newspaper:

> TO ALL RIDERS OF THE MONTGOMERY BUS TRANSPORTATION LINES
>
> Bus service will be halted on Thursday, December 22, 1955, for all bus riders of transportation lines. Such service will be discontinued throughout the Christmas holiday season. There will be no buses operating on any lines in the city or county in the area. Even the bus drivers deserve a holiday period.
>
> (Signed) The Bus Company Manager

Most importantly, when the public transportation service stopped for the Christmas holidays, white bus riders had no way to get to the shopping areas, for whites who rode buses usually had limited funds and no money for taxi service. Of necessity they had to do without some things. Thus, willy-nilly, they were boycotting, too. They did not buy, but it was not intentional!

The merchants began to feel the squeeze. Some businesses began closing or going bankrupt. "Closed" was

seen on many storefronts where "Open for Business" had been seen before.

The truth was that the buses had no riders, and the bus company was financially distressed. The company had survived from December 5 until December 22, about seventeen days, almost without passengers. Following the holidays, service resumed on routes in basically white areas, but the continuing loss of revenue was tremendous.

According to [bus company manager] Mr. [James H.] Bagley, eight lines were completely discontinued. Thirty-nine bus drivers were laid off or dismissed when service

The lack of riders during the boycott became a hardship for the bus company. (Grey Villet/ Getty Images.)

was first cut. Dozens of the huge transit vehicles sat lined up in the car lot at the northern end of McDonough Street. There was no need for them. One day passersby saw the giant buses being used to help a private company pack down some newly built-up ground. The few buses still in operation underwent route cuts and changes and ran much less frequently than the previous seven-and-a-half-minute intervals.

According to the black bus company workers, there had never been more than four Negroes working in all. According to one of them, they held the general "flunky" jobs such as "handy" men. However, when the wholesale layoffs began, the black men were among the first to go, for whites who had tenure took over their menial jobs. Regular drivers chose to become flunkies or handymen rather than go without work altogether.

When these black workers were dismissed, the kindly Mr. Bagley interceded with other firms to get three of them placed in other jobs. He spoke well of them and expressed regret that they had to be laid off.

An Example of Commitment

One December day a very aged black woman, who was struggling along on foot, walking with a cane, was overtaken by a bus with a lone black rider on it. The bus stopped at the stop sign just ahead of the old woman, to let the black passenger out. Seeing the situation, the crippled woman hobbled along faster toward the bus. The driver, thinking that the woman was hurrying to get on, seized the opportunity to show how courteous he could be to black people if they would only ride again. So he called out, in a very friendly tone, "Don't hurt yourself, auntie, I'll wait for you!"

With anger and scorn, the old woman pantingly, gaspingly called up to him as she hurried past the open bus door, "I'm not your auntie, and I don't want to get on your bus. I'm trying to catch that n----- who just got off!"

Then she drew back her cane to strike the rider as he fled beyond her reach.

So at Christmas, when there should have been peace and good will on earth, there was in Montgomery each race's suspicion of the other. There was no open demonstration of this suspicion, but one could see it in the sharp glances that followed persons as they passed each other on the streets, in stores, or at the laundry. In crowded elevators, where Negro and white rubbed shoulders, or in lines at the post office or bank, the chill was there. The suspicion!

Since the bus company management had given the bus drivers and their empty buses a holiday, buses no longer rattled by as people walked along in the biting cold and rain, carrying heavy bundles of food and practical needs in their arms. Everybody knew that it would be a long time before black people again rode the buses. But nobody anticipated at the start that another full year would pass before the situation was resolved.

In mid-December 1955 the black people of Montgomery were calm, proud, content, and strangely peaceful. They faced the birthday of Christ with grim determination to continue their passive resistance.

> Many of the boycotters vowed never to ride the bus again, integrated or not!

And then came Christmas Day!

On this holiday, December 25, 1955, a long paid advertisement from the MIA [Montgomery Improvement Association] appeared in the local papers. The ad explained the purpose of the organization, the position it had taken in connection with the boycott, the fairness of the black citizens' request for improved seating conditions. It spoke of the human dignity of all mankind, and of the need for a better understanding among all peoples, especially among the races. Its tone was conciliatory, but the article assured readers that black people of

Montgomery would never, of their own free will, return to the buses without positive improvements. The ad ended with a prayer for peace on earth and good will to all mankind.

Headlines blazed the Negro protest across the pages of large newspapers around the world. There seemed hardly a spot on the globe where civilization extends that did not carry the news. According to hundreds of reports from reporters who represented large newspapers and magazines across the world and who visited Montgomery, oppressed people the world over took heart and became more optimistic that their own fate could be improved.

Black Montgomerians took heart, too. They no longer complained of exhaustion after long walks. As the City Fathers remained obstinate in their resolve not to yield to the blacks' requests, many of the boycotters vowed never to ride the bus again, integrated or not!

The Memories of a Twelve-Year-Old Montgomery Girl

Jannell McGrew

Those most directly affected by the Montgomery Bus Boycott were those who relied on the buses to get to work. But the event affected the children of Montgomery as well. In the following selection, Gwen Patton, who was only twelve years old during the boycott, remembers the participation of both her family and herself in the event. While her parents helped to raise money and awareness, Patton went to regular mass meetings and recalled many people walking with an air of both happiness and dignity.

Their framed smiling faces cover the length of one of her bedroom walls.

The memories in black-and-white and some in color stare into space from a time long passed.

They are her memories, her past and what has helped shape her today. Pictures of her mother, father, her grandparents, and her friends.

And Gwen Patton remembers those days, the good and the bad. She clearly recalls the days of the Montgomery Bus Boycott. She was just a girl when she put her hands and mind to work for a cause that took lives. She even wrote a paper on the era, a time she'll not soon forget.

It was just months after Rosa Parks was arrested on Dec. 1, 1955, for refusing to give up her bus seat to a white passenger. Patton was aware of what had happened.

Her father, C. Robert Patton Sr., was much engaged in helping to raise money to support the boycott.

In April 1956, four months after Parks' famous arrest, a young Gwen came to Montgomery and helped raise money.

At 12 years old, she didn't have the right to vote, but she understood what it meant to fight for that right.

She remembers the citizenship classes her grandparents, Mary Jane Patton and Sam Patton Sr., had in their homes.

There were civic leagues all over town trying to beat back Jim Crow laws [segregating blacks and whites]. Blacks studied hard to pass literacy tests designed to keep them from registering to vote.

Patton recalls her grandmother telling her and other youngsters to ride in the back of the bus to watch the scenery.

"I never knew that I could not sit on the front of the bus," she said.

Small Protests and Contributions

But one day, she discovered the difference between black rights and white rights. She was in a store sitting down and a white clerk called her a "pickaninny," a racial slur. Patton didn't know what that word was, but she felt it was wrong, and she reacted and poured out liquid in the store.

"That was my first conscious protest," she said with a smile.

She remembers other things that were done to financially support the boycott: bake sales, little competitions like that between neighborhood women.

"It was just a little competition to help underwrite the boycott," Patton said.

Her father also had fund-raisers and he would send tools to her grandfather, a contractor, who suffered retribution from whites who refused to do contracting business with him during the boycott.

But, Patton pointed out, reprisals did not stop their determination.

"I was convinced we were going to win," she said.

> 'I was convinced we were going to win.'

She attended as many mass meetings as her little feet could go to. Every Monday night, she recalled, it was "Monday motivation."

"You were truly motivated at the Monday mass meetings," she said, describing the churches as "movement centers."

The houses of worship were not only for solace of the spirit, Patton explained, they were disseminators of information, the hubs of strategic planning and the think-tanks of the movement.

She recalled all the walking.

"Three hundred and eighty-one days, people walked, walked with joy," Patton said. "Over our heads, we saw freedom in the air."

Freedom indeed came, after the U.S. Supreme Court desegregated public transportation systems.

But her grandmother, the woman who told her to ride in the back to catch the scenery, curiously enough, continued to sit in the back of the bus.

Patton was puzzled, and she confronted her matriarch about her actions, asking why she continued to ride in the back when people—when she herself—had struggled to gain the right to ride without being relegated to back of a segregated bus.

Her grandmother's answer: She didn't struggle just to be able to ride up front with the whites. She fought to be able to ride anywhere she wanted to on that bus or any other bus.

Patton's back straightened with pride: "This movement was not about white people. This movement was about yourself."

CHRONOLOGY

1896   In the *Plessy v. Ferguson* decision, the US Supreme Court determines that states and municipalities can create "separate but equal" facilities for blacks and whites. The decision legalizes segregation and validates Jim Crow laws that many states would establish to keep blacks and whites separate in places ranging from buses to restaurants to water fountains.

1943   Rosa Parks, a Montgomery, Alabama, activist and secretary of the local branch of the NAACP (National Association for the Advancement of Colored People), is forced off a city bus for refusing to observe local Jim Crow rules.

1953   June: A bus boycott in Baton Rouge, Louisiana, ends with a compromise granting black riders new privileges.

1954   May 17: The US Supreme Court, in *Brown v. Board of Education*, holds that segregation in schools is not constitutional. The decision becomes a precedent for fighting Jim Crow laws elsewhere.

        May 21: Jo Ann Robinson, a Montgomery professor and head of the Women's Political Council of African American activists, writes a letter to Montgomery's mayor, warning him of the possibility of a bus boycott.

1955   March 2: Montgomery teenager Claudette Colvin is arrested for refusing to abandon her seat on a bus.

October 21: Mary Louise Smith is arrested for disobeying segregation on Montgomery's buses.

December 1: Rosa Parks refuses to abandon her seat on a Montgomery bus and is arrested.

December 2: Jo Ann Robinson and other Montgomery activists, including E.D. Dixon and Fred Gray, plan a boycott of Montgomery buses.

December 5: The Montgomery Bus Boycott begins. It is intended, at first, to last one day only.

Rosa Parks is convicted and fined.

A group of Montgomery leaders and activists, led by Reverends Martin Luther King Jr. and Ralph David Abernathy, start the Montgomery Improvement Association (MIA) and expand the boycott.

December 8: In the first of a series of fruitless talks, MIA leaders and officials from Montgomery and the private bus company are unable to reach a compromise to end the boycott.

December 13: The MIA begins a carpool system to help boycotters get back and forth to work and other destinations.

1956   January: Rosa Parks loses her job at the Montgomery Fair department store.

January 30: Martin Luther King Jr.'s Montgomery home is attacked with bombs. Although some activists want to respond with violence, King convinces them that their protest must be nonviolent.

February 1: The court challenge to segregation on Montgomery's buses, *Browder v. Gayle*, is filed by MIA attorney Fred Gray.

February 10: A so-called White Citizens Council holds a massive rally in Montgomery at which city leaders pledge to uphold segregation.

February 21: Many MIA activists, including Parks and King, are charged with violating an Alabama state anti-boycott law as events in Montgomery draw increasing attention from around the nation. King is eventually convicted and fined, although no others are tried.

June 5: An Alabama federal court delivers its decision in *Browder v. Gayle*. The three-judge panel decides two-to-one that segregation on buses is unconstitutional. Montgomery's white leaders immediately appeal the decision to the US Supreme Court as the boycott continues.

August 25: The Montgomery home of pastor Robert Graetz, a white member of the MIA, is bombed.

November 13: The US Supreme Court upholds the *Browder v. Gayle* decision, making segregation on Montgomery's buses illegal.

November 14: Montgomery activists and the MIA vote unanimously to end the boycott once the Supreme Court's decision is implemented.

December 21: After the Supreme Court's decision is formally implemented on December 20, the Montgomery Bus Boycott comes to an end.

December 23–31: Episodes of violence, including gunshots fired at buses and King's home, follow the end of the boycott.

1957   January: The Southern Christian Leadership Conference (SCLC) is formed, with Martin Luther King Jr., at its head. The organization plays a leading role in the civil rights movement over the next years.

1963   A bus boycott in Bristol, England, inspired by events in Montgomery, helps to lift Britain's "colour bar" of segregation.

1964   President Lyndon B. Johnson signs a broad Civil Rights Act. It bans segregation in all public places, thereby bringing a formal end to Jim Crow.

1968   April 4: Martin Luther King Jr. is assassinated in Memphis, Tennessee.

1996   Rosa Parks is awarded the Presidential Medal of Freedom by President Bill Clinton.

1999   *Time* magazine names Rosa Parks one of the twenty most influential people of the twentieth century.

2005   October 25: Rosa Parks dies in Detroit, Michigan.

FOR FURTHER READING

Books

Ralph David Abernathy, *And the Walls Came Tumbling Down: An Autobiography*. New York: Harper and Row, 1989.

Tayor Branch, *Parting the Waters: America in the King Years, 1954–1963*. New York: Simon and Schuster, 1988.

Douglas Brinkley, *Rosa Parks*. New York: Viking/Penguin Putnam, 2000.

John Hope Franklin, *From Slavery to Freedom*. New York: Alfred A. Knopf, 1947.

Russell Freedman, *Freedom Walkers: The Story of the Montgomery Bus Boycott*. New York: Holiday House, 2008.

David J. Garrow, *Bearing the Cross: Martin Luther King, Jr. and the Southern Christian Leadership Conference*. New York: William Morrow, 1986.

David J. Garrow, ed., *The Walking City: The Montgomery Bus Boycott, 1955–1956*. New York: Carlson Publishing, 1989.

Fred Gray, *Bus Ride to Justice*. Montgomery: Black Belt Press, 1995.

Steven Kasher, *The Civil Rights Movement: A Photographic History, 1954–68*. New York: Abbeville Press, 1996.

Herbert Kohl and Marian Wright Edelman, *She Would Not be Moved: How We Tell the Story of Rosa Parks and the Montgomery Bus Boycott*. New York: New Press, 2007.

Martin Luther King Jr., *Stride Toward Freedom*. New York: Harper, 1958.

Aldon D. Morris, *The Origins of the Civil Rights Movement*. New York: Free Press, 1984.

Rosa Parks with Jim Haskins, *Rosa Parks: My Story*. New York: Dial Books, 1992.

Jo Ann Robinson, *The Montgomery Bus Boycott and the Women Who Started It: The Memoir of Jo Ann Gibson Robinson*. Knoxville: University of Tennesee Press, 1987.

C. Vann Woodward, *The Strange Career of Jim Crow*. New York: Oxford University Press, 1974.

Periodicals

Kazembe Balagun, "Learning From Rosa Parks," *The Indypendent*, November 9, 2005.

Rupert Cornwell, "Rosa Parks: An American Hero," *The Independent* (UK), October 26, 2005.

Charlene Crowell, "Dr. King and the 1955–1956 Montgomery Bus Boycott," *Milwaukee Courier*, January 22, 2011.

Globe and Mail (Toronto), "Driving the road to freedom," December 3, 2005.

Jesse Jackson, "Parks Liberated the South: End of Segregation Made Us One Nation," *Syracuse Herald-Journal*, June 21, 1999.

Sam Roberts, "1955: moving to the front of the bus: during the Montgomery bus boycott, blacks used their wallets as weapons in the struggle for civil rights," *New York Times Upfront*, November 14, 2005.

Time, "The South: Battle of the Buses," June 18, 1956.

Juan Williams, "The Long History of a Bus Ride," *New York Times*, November 1, 2005.

Websites

The King Center (www.thekingcenter.org). Established in 1968 by Coretta Scott King, the King Center is the official memorial dedicated to the legacy of Martin Luther King Jr. Its website offers access to pictures, video and audio clips, and general information on King.

Rosa Parks Museum (http://montgomery.troy.edu/rosaparks/museum). Troy University in Montgomery, Alabama, maintains a museum devoted to Rosa Parks. This website provides general information on Parks and the boycott, as well as photographs and information on museum exhibits.

The Story of the Montgomery Bus Boycott (www. montgomeryboycott.com). This website of the *Montgomery Advertiser* newspaper provides a thorough exploration of the boycott, with links to interviews, contemporary newspaper articles, and video clips.

Unseen. Unforgotten. (www.al.com/unseen). This website of the *Birmingham News*, the *Huntsville Times*, and the *Mobile Press-Register* maintains a page providing articles, photographs, and links on the bus boycott and other civil rights efforts in Alabama.

INDEX

Y

Z